Mir Osman Ali Khan, Nizam VII of Hyderabad
(born 1886, ruled 1911-48)

The Nocturnal Court

Darbaar-e-Dürbaar

The Nocturnal Court
Darbaar-e-Dūrbaar
The Life of a Prince of Hyderabad

Sidq Jaisi

Translated from Urdu
With an Introduction and Notes
by

Narendra Luther

OXFORD
UNIVERSITY PRESS

OXFORD
UNIVERSITY PRESS

YMCA Library Building, Jai Singh Road, New Delhi 110 001

Oxford University Press is a department of the University of Oxford. It furthers the
University's objective of excellence in research, scholarship, and education
by publishing worldwide in

Oxford   New York

Auckland   Cape Town   Dar es Salaam   Hong Kong   Karachi   Kuala Lumpur
Madrid   Melbourne   Mexico City   Nairobi   New Delhi   Shanghai   Taipei   Toronto

With offices in

Argentina   Austria   Brazil   Chile   Czech Republic   France   Greece   Guatemala
Hungary   Italy   Japan   Poland   Portugal   Singapore   South Korea   Switzerland
Thailand   Turkey   Ukraine   Vietnam

Oxford is a registered trademark of Oxford University Press
in the UK and in certain other countries

Published in India by Oxford University Press, New Delhi

© Oxford University Press 2004

The moral rights of the authors have been asserted
Database right Oxford University Press (maker)

First Published 2004
Fourth impression 2010

ISBN-13: 978-0-19-566605-2
ISBN-10: 0-19-566605-4

Typeset in Garamond by Le Studio Graphique, Gurgaon 122 001
Printed in India by Rajshri Photolithographers, Delhi 110 032
Published by Oxford University Press
YMCA Library Building, Jai Singh Road, New Delhi 110 001

THE NOCTURNAL COURT

Contents

The Nocturnal Court
(*Darbaar-e-Dürbaar* by Sidq Jaisi)

Photographs

Acknowledgements

I CAME ACROSS the book *Darbaar-e-Dürbaar* in Urdu during the course of my research for my book *Memoirs of a City* (Orient Longman, 1995). Written by Sidq Jaisi, it struck me as a most interesting eyewitness account of life in the court of the second son of the last Nizam of Hyderabad. Moreover, it also described, in a sort of gestalt, life outside the court. It evoked a nostalgia because that Hyderabad is no more. It threw an arc light on the feudal society of Hyderabad, which was replicated in varying degrees, as the generality of feudalism anywhere. I then decided to translate the book from Urdu into English so that a wider section of the public could have access to this interesting account. However, I myself needed some clarifications about some of the persons and the pet names of the courtiers used by Prince Muazzam Jah in his court. There is a dearth of published material on the subject. There is a short biography of the author, Mir Tassaduq Hussain, Sidq Jaisi by Mohammad Nooruddin Khan.[1] One doctoral thesis on Fani by Professor Mughani Tabassum and one on Maharaja Kishen Pershad by Professor Habeeb Zia were kindly made available to me by the scholars themselves. The then librarian of Osmania University, Mrs Dorothy Isaar, was good enough to make available to me the unpublished Ph.D. thesis of Mohamed Abdul Khader Imadi on 'The Nobles of Hyderabad', completed in 1977. Some scattered material could be found in the stray articles and memoirs of various persons in magazines both in India and Pakistan. However, most of the material lay in the heads and hearts of persons.

The first draft of the book was ready in 1994. Since then, a number of other commitments prevented me from revising and refining it. Last year, a scholar friend happened to see it and said that I must pull it out and make it available to the public to have a peep into the romantic past.

When I took up the project, most of the persons mentioned in the book were no more. However, there were still some persons who had either seen the court themselves or had heard first-hand accounts of it from those who attended it. There was thus a considerable oral tradition on the subject.

I would like to express my gratitude to the following persons who agreed to talk to me and answer my queries, and who cleared my doubts on many points: the late Nawab Kazim Jung Bahadur (Ali Pasha), son-in-law of the seventh Nizam, and thus a brother-in-law of the Prince; Mrs Bilkees Latif, who knew Princess Niloufer, with whom she came in close contact when her husband Air Chief Marshall Latif was India's ambassador to France and Niloufer was staying in Paris; Syed Farkhonda Ali Khan, brother-in-law of Ali Pasha; Colonel Khusro Yar Khan of the Hyderabad army and later of the Indian Army. Of the poets, Khwaja Hussain Sharief 'Shouq' was a friend of the Prince; the late Syed Abid Ali 'Syeed Shaheedi' was the son of Nawab Shaheed Yar Jung who had served as Comptroller of the Household of the Prince and so had heard some accounts from his father. The late Khumar Barabankvi, the renowned poet and lyricist of the Hindi film industry, spared an evening during one of his visits to Hyderabad to throw some light on the character, and to give an account of the last days of the Prince. The late Ghulam Hyder of the Indian Administrative Service (IAS), and Mrs Sabeeha Najaf Ali Khan (whose husband was also in the IAS) who had a formidable library which she tends with a rare devotion, also provided some useful bits of information and clarifications. M.A. Hadi and Syed Azizul Hasan of HEH the Nizam's Trust were good enough to provide useful information about the numerous trusts set up by the Nizam.

I must include in this list all the friends, living or dead, who contributed to the oral history references of my previous book *Memoirs of a City*, of which this book is really an offspring. Some helped me in various ways on condition of anonymity, so they are not mentioned here, but I would like to let them know that I remember them.

None of the persons mentioned above is, however, in any way responsible for any elaboration or interpretation in the notes made in the book.

I also acknowledge the help and guidance given by that personification of modesty, the late Mehboob Hussain Jigar, Joint Editor of the *Siasat* Urdu daily. He always knew who would know what and how much on the old Hyderabad. M.A. Samad of the Urdu Research Centre has a head full of stories, as his house is full of books. He gave me a good deal of background information and published references in Urdu. For permission to get some relevant pictures, I am indebted to the former Commissioner of State Archives, Dr S.K. Pachauri.

I owe a debt of gratitude to Professor K.C. Kanda, who has done a lot of work on introducing the best of Urdu poets and poetry through a number of his books. He very kindly vetted my translation of the Urdu couplets in the book.

In conclusion, I thank my numerous friends who, by merely repeating their inquiries about the progress of the book, spurred me on.

Hyderabad NARENDRA LUTHER

Notes

[1] *Sidq Jaisi* by Mohammad Nooruddin Khan (Hyderabad, Adabistan-e-Deccan, 1994).

Foreword

THE OPULENCE OF THE LIVES of kings, potentates, and nobles is beyond the imagination of common people like us, so distant, separate, and strange is it from our lives. Their living style, food and drink, joys and sorrows, loves and hates, interests and hobbies, indulgences and sports, their treatment of relations and those close to them, their ceremonials connected with births and deaths, their generosities and largesse, their cruelties, their worship, their festivities, their day and night—all are larger than life, technicolour, and extraordinary.

There has been a need for someone to enter their forbidden territory, to savour their company, share their lifestyle, and make others privy to it through the written word. Two conditions are necessary for a person to undertake such a task. First, he should know his subject well—he should be a real insider. Second, whatever he writes should be authentic to the best of his knowledge and belief, and free of judgemental bias.

Sidq Jaisi is ideally qualified to undertake the task. A man of letters, Sidq not only sports a pen name that spells truth; he has in fact lived up to that epithet (Sidq means 'truth' in Urdu). He is not concerned with praise or ridicule. His aim is to paint a faithful picture. Providence took him to a court like that of the Deccan. He stayed there for several years and was able to observe it closely. Apparently, he wanted to write as a contemporary poet and about his days as a courtier. But Fate had a different design. Consciously or unconsciously, he ended up writing the full account of the court of the Junior Prince of the Nizam. Thus he has, at once, rendered a valuable service both to literature and history. This book, though not bulky, contains within itself a world of meaning. It has something for everybody—poets, writers, critics, biographers, historians. The lucidity of Sidq's writing is such that once you pick up the book, you don't want to put it down. The narration makes facts appear like fiction.

Daryabad, Barabanki   ABDUL MAJID DARYABADI[1]
14 April 1960

Notes

[1] Born in 1892 in Uttar Pradesh, he graduated from Canning College, Lucknow. He worked in the Bureau of Translation of Osmania University during 1917–18, and visited Hyderabad in 1938 and 1963. He was a commentator on the Quran and a writer, journalist, and columnist known for his elegant style. His book *Taasuraat-e-Deccan* (Memoirs of the Deccan) was published in Pakistan.

Genealogical Tree of the Asif Jahi Dynasty

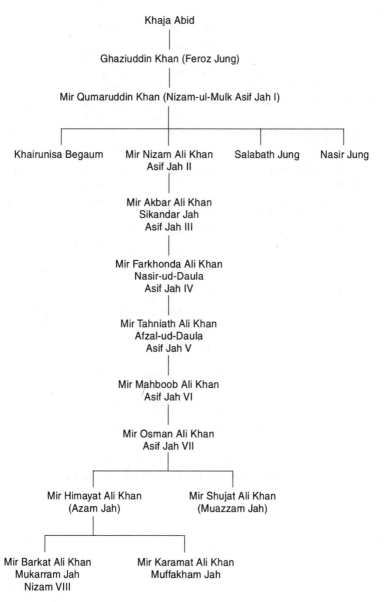

Khaja Abid

Ghaziuddin Khan (Feroz Jung)

Mir Qumaruddin Khan (Nizam-ul-Mulk Asif Jah I)

Khairunisa Begaum   Mir Nizam Ali Khan
Asif Jah II   Salabath Jung   Nasir Jung

Mir Akbar Ali Khan
Sikandar Jah
Asif Jah III

Mir Farkhonda Ali Khan
Nasir-ud-Daula
Asif Jah IV

Mir Tahniath Ali Khan
Afzal-ud-Daula
Asif Jah V

Mir Mahboob Ali Khan
Asif Jah VI

Mir Osman Ali Khan
Asif Jah VII

Mir Himayat Ali Khan
(Azam Jah)   Mir Shujat Ali Khan
(Muazzam Jah)

Mir Barkat Ali Khan
Mukarram Jah
Nizam VIII   Mir Karamat Ali Khan
Muffakham Jah

Asif[*] Jahi Rulers of Hyderabad

	Date of Birth	Ruled [†]	Died
Mir Qumaruddin Khan Asif Jah I	11-7-1671	31-7-1720 to 1748	22-5-1748
** Mir Ahmed Alikhan Nasir Jung Nizam ud Daula	15-2-1712	23-5-1748 to 1750	5-12-1750
** Hidath Mohiuddin Khan Muzafar Jung		5-12-1750 to 1751	3-2-1751
** Syed Mohammed Khan Amir ul Mulk Salabath Jung	1718	3-2-1751 to 1762	11-9-1763
Nizam Ali Khan Nizam ul Mulk Asif Jah II	24-2-1734	8-7-1762 to 1803	6-8-1803
Mir Akbar Ali Khan Sikander Jah Asif Jah III	11-11-1768	11-8-1803 to 1829	21-5-1829
Mir Farkhonda Ali Khan Nasir ud Daula Asif Jah IV	25-4-1794	23-5-1829 to 1857	17-5-1857
Mir Tahniath Ali Khan Afzal ud Daula Asif Jah V	11-10-1827	18-5-1857 to 1869	26-2-1869
Mir Mahboob Ali Khan Asif Jah VI	17-8-1866	29-2-1869 to 1911	29-8-1911
Mir Osman Ali Khan Asif Jah VII	5-4-1886	18-9-1911 to 1948	24-2-1967

[*] The correct term is 'Asaf'. But different authorities have used the term 'Asif'. We have followed the same practice.

[†] The year of end of rule is the same as year of death except in the case of the last Nizam where both dates are given.

[**] These three rulers are not enumerated in the serial order of the Asif Jahs mainly because they were not granted the title of Asif Jah.

Ref. The Chronology of Modern Hyderabad 1720–1890 (Central Record Office, Hyderabad Government, 1954, p. 326).

Hyderabad State

Introduction

DESCRIPTIONS OF THE GRANDEUR of the Mughal court, which attained its apogee under Shah Jahan (ruled 1628–58) abound. The Red Fort at Delhi with its exquisite Peacock Throne represented a pinnacle never again to be equalled. Accounts of the later Mughals, however, are as much about decadence and debauchery as pomp and grandeur.[1]

The people of Delhi gave Mohammad Shah (ruled 1719–48) the nickname of 'Rangeela'—the merry one. Nadir Shah, the Iranian invader, sacked Delhi in 1739 and noted the degeneracy of the Emperor and his court. Nadir Shah halted his massacre of the populace of Delhi at the intercession of the aged and sagacious Prime Minister of the Mughal empire, Mir Qamaruddin. The Iranian invader, impressed by him, offered the throne of India to him, whom he found the only noble fit to rule. The old Prime Minister declined the offer, saying that he could not betray the Mughal emperor.

The revelry of the later Mughals was revived under the brief rule of Wajid Ali Shah, the last ruler of Avadh (ruled 1848–57). Wajid Ali's father, a devout Muslim, gave him a religious education hoping to make him a pious ruler. But Wajid's natural inclination was towards architecture, poetry, and music. He also liked the company of women. He took debauchery to artistic heights. He built buildings, wrote poetry, and composed *ragas*. He created a women's brigade which would participate in regular drills, like its male counterparts.

He built Qaisar Bagh, which accommodated the royal palaces surrounded by the nobles' residences. The gate leading to Qaisar Bagh was called Chou Lakhi because it had cost Rs 400,000 to build. Once a year, a fair was held in the compound of Qaisar Bagh. In this, he used to play the role of the Hindu mythological hero Krishna and have women dance with him as *gopis*. Common people were allowed to attend if they came dressed in red ochre clothes. There was much revelry at this fair. Sometimes the king would become a *yogi*—mendicant—putting on a mendicant's robes and smearing his face with ash made of ground pearls.

The various regiments of his army were given frivolous names like Banka (Dandy), Tirchha (Fop), and Ghanghur (Dark). Infantry battalions too were given such names as Akhtari (lucky) and Nadiri (rare). Women of varying backgrounds sang the ragas composed by the king and danced to their tune. The king too joined in the revelries. He thus came to surround himself with men and women of undesirable character and taste. The affairs of state were completely neglected.

The British then deposed him and exiled him to Calcutta (now Kolkata) on an annual pension of Rs 1.2 million. He was given a piece of land in Garden Beach. It was an earthen mound, and thus came to be called Matiya Burj in Urdu. There he developed a new township, which was held to be better than Lucknow. It had a population of 40,000 living largely on the income derived by the exiled ruler from the British.

The degenerate splendour of his court was documented by the Urdu writer and journalist Abdul Halim Sharar (1860–1926) in a series of essays under the title: *Hindustan Mein Mahsriqi Tammdun ka Akhri Namuna* (The Last Example of Oriental Culture in India).[2] According to Sharar, Wajid Ali Shah's 'era forms the last page of the history of this eastern court and the last stanza of the old elegy'. Wajid Ali Shah was a Shia Muslim. He reconciled the demands of his sect with his natural predilection in a very amusing manner. One cannot do better than describe the situation in the words of Sharar himself:

There was the same desire for collecting good-looking women and concentrating on beauty and love in Matiya Burj as one hears there had been in Lucknow. In Matiya Burj, however, when embarking on these desires, due regard was given to religious considerations. The King belonged to the Shia sect of Islam, and according to Shia law, *mutta*,[3] temporary marriage, is legal. Taking advantage of this religious freedom, the King pursued his inclinations to his heart's content. He made it his rule not to look at a woman who was not temporarily married to him, and carried his religious caution to such lengths that he even entered into a temporary marriage with a young female water-carrier who would pass him when she was carrying water to the women's quarters; he gave her the title of Nawab Ab Rasan Begum, Her Highness the Lady Water-Provider. There was also a young sweeping-woman who used to come into his presence. She too joined the ranks of the temporarily married and was honoured with the title of Nawab Musafa Begam, the Lady Purifier. In the same way, the enjoyment of music was also confined to those women who belonged to him. It was very seldom that a courtesan danced before the King. These temporarily married women were formed into various groups and taught diverse forms of dancing and singing. The following are the names of some of these groups: Radha Manzil, Sardha Manzil, Jhumar ('Earring'), Latkan ('Dwindling'), Nath ('Nose ring'), Ghunghat ('Veil'), Rahas ('Dance'), and Naqal ('Mime'). There were scores of similar groups who had been given the best instruction in the dancing and singing in which the King delighted. He had entered into temporary wedlock with all of them and they were called Begams. In some of these groups, a few young girls had not yet reached the age of puberty. They were not in a state of temporary wedlock and they would be admitted to that state immediately on reaching puberty. Most lived near the King in Sultan Khana but some of them lived in separate women's apartments in other houses. Those temporarily married women who bore children were given the title of Mahal. They were given separate women's apartments as their residences, received enhanced allowances, and were greatly honoured.

However, Sharar hastens to the defence of Wajid Ali Shah. He adds in the next paragraph:

From what has been written above, it is clearly evident that, except for music,[4] the King was in every way extremely devout, abstinent and a strict observer of Muslim religious law. He never missed offering up his prayers. He observed the fast for the whole of thirty days in the month of Ramadan. He was a life-long abstainer from opium, wine and other intoxicants and he performed the mourning ceremonies at the time of Muharram with sincere devotion.[5]

Of course, Wajid Ali Shah was not the only one of the Indian princes of his time to live a life of such unbounded libertinism. But no Sharar recorded the happenings elsewhere. Later in the middle of the twentieth century, men like K.L. Gauba and Diwan Jarmani Das wrote about the scandalous private lives of some of the Indian princes. Of these, the latter could claim personal knowledge of the subject since he had served under some of the princes. However, these accounts were intended more to titillate than to enlighten. *Lives of the Indian Princes* by Charles Allen and Sharada Dwivedi, *The Maharajas of India* by Ann Morrow, and *Plain Tales from the Raj* by Charles Allen are sober accounts of the lives of the Indian princes. But they paint essentially the same picture. They bear out the comment made by Rudyard Kipling that 'Providence created the maharajas to offer mankind a spectacle' of jewels and marble palaces. One might add that they were also intended to show how far luxurious living could go to cross the limits of depravity. The princes had not only power without responsibility, but also pleasures without limit.

There is no extant account of the life of an Indian court after Sharar's narration of Wajid Ali's rule. Nizam Rampuri has reportedly written a disparaging account of the Rampur court. Yagana Changezi, the poet, has also touched upon the subject in his autobiography. But these books are no longer available. In that situation, the account of the life of the Junior Prince of Hyderabad, Mir Muazzam Jah, written by Mirza Tassaduq Hussain, Sidq Jaisi in 1961 remains the one representative document on the subject. Therein lies its importance.

Mohammad Quli, the fifth and most celebrated ruler of the Qutb Shahi dynasty (ruled 1580–1611), moved out of the fort city of Golconda, and founded a new city as the capital of the sultanate. He gave it the name of Bhagnagar after his beloved Bhagmati. In course of time, it came to be called Hyderabad. It was a well-planned city and became renowned for its beauty and greenery. Contemporary accounts rated it as bigger and better than Agra and Lahore—the great cities of the Mughals.

The Nizams of Hyderabad

Golconda was conquered by the Mughal emperor, Aurangzeb in 1687 after a prolonged siege of the fort lasting eight months. It was made a part of the Deccan *Suba*—the southern province of the Mughals.

Here it will be pertinent to give a background of the Nizams of Hyderabad.

Khwaja Abid, Qazi of Bokhara, and a remote descendant of the second Caliph of Islam, Abu Bakr, passed through India on his way to Mecca in 1655. Because of his reputed scholarship, the Mughal emperor Shahjahan honoured him and offered him a job. He promised to accept it on his return from his pilgrimage. However, by the time he returned, the whole situation had changed. At Agra, Prince Dara was running the government on behalf of the ailing emperor. Aurangzeb had laid siege to Bijapur. Abid could not go to Agra. He therefore proceeded to Bijapur and joined Aurangzeb. On winning the war of succession and becoming emperor, Aurangzeb appointed him in a high job, and conferred the title of Qilij Khan meaning a master swordsman. He was with Aurangzeb during the siege of Golconda in 1687 where a shell fired from within the fort killed him.

His son, Shahabuddin had joined him from Samarkand in 1669. Aurangzeb gave him the mansab of 300 Horse. A son was born to him in 1671 and the Emperor named him Qamaruddin. When he was six, a mansab of 400 Horse was granted to him. At twenty, the Emperor gave him the title of Chin Qilij (young swordsman) and a mansab of 4000 Horse.

Shahabuddin won many honours during the reign of Aurangzeb. He was given the title of Ghaziuddin Feroz Jung. He was the commander of the Mughal forces during the siege of Golconda. Due to the outbreak of plague in Bijapur, Shahabuddin lost his eyesight. In spite of that disability, he was kept in service and was the Governor of Berar at the time of Aurangzeb's death in 1707.

The First Nizam

Qamaruddin fought many campaigns for the Mughal emperor Aurangzeb. In 1702, he was appointed Governor of Bijapur. During the wars of succession that followed Aurangzeb's death, Qamaruddin remained neutral. He was respected for his valour and sagacity and was much sought after by the successive occupants and claimants to the throne of Delhi. Tired of court intrigues, he resigned from his job and went into a retreat. In 1712, Farrukhsiyar, upon becoming emperor, conferred the title of Nizam-ul-Mulk on him and appointed him Governor of the Deccan. He was instrumental in finishing off the infamous Sayyed Brothers, the kingmakers of Delhi.

Much against his will, the dissolute and irresolute Mughal emperor Bahadur Shah Rangeela—the Merrymaker—appointed Qamaruddin, as Prime Minister in 1722. He thus came to hold two offices: that of the Prime Minister of the Empire, and the Governor of the Deccan. Not being able to set matters right in the court, he set out for the Deccan. Meanwhile, in a double-crossing move, Bahadur Shah appointed Mubariz Khan as the Governor of the Deccan. Qamaruddin defeated Mubariz Khan at the Battle of Shakkarkhed in 1724 and regained his charge. The Mughal emperor made an apparent show of happiness at this *fait accompli*, and conferred the title of 'Asaf Jah' on him. This title derives from the name of Asaf, the Biblical King Solomon's minister, who was renowned for his wisdom and sagacity.[6]

As the legend goes, on his way to the Deccan, during one of his hunts, Qamaruddin lost his way in a jungle. Hungry, thirsty, and woe-begone, he happened to come upon the cottage of a hermit. All that the sage could offer him were loaves of round dry baked bread—*kulcha*—and plain water. The exhausted noble had his full and in spite of the host's insistence, he could eat no more than seven kulchas. The hermit then said that since he had eaten seven kulchas, his family would rule for seven generations.

The legend goes further that in recognition of this benediction, the Nizam incorporated the symbol of the kulcha in his flag. However, the Nizam himself contradicted this. According to his anecdotes recorded by his chief secretary, Lala Mansa Ram, the Nizam clarified that the symbol on the flag did not represent kulcha, but the moon. That was because 'my name Qamaruddin means the moon of my faith',[7] But so strong was the legend that as late as 1899, the sixth Nizam approved the modified design of the flag observing that the circular symbol stood for kulcha.[8]

Because of his titles—Nizam-ul-Mulk and Asaf Jah—he is referred to as the first Nizam, and the first Asaf Jah. Due to the latter title, he is known as the founder of the Asaf Jahi dynasty, which dates from his resumption of the governorship of the Deccan in 1724.

The Mughal emperor Mohammad Shah summoned him for help when Nadir Shah invaded India in 1737. Later, it was at his intervention that the massacre of Delhi ordered by Nadir Shah was stopped. The Iranian invader was so impressed by his sagacity that he offered him the throne of Delhi saying that he was the only fit person to rule India. He, however, gratefully declined the offer lest he should be guilty of treachery to his master.

The first Nizam died in 1748 after a life crowded with glory. In a life spanning 79 years, he saw the reign of seven Mughal emperors and fought 87 battles. Though their viceroy, in fact he was more powerful than the emperors. He made appointments, granted *jagirs*, and dispensed favours according to his own whim and fancy. He had the British and the French seeking favours from him in their struggle to establish supremacy in India.

Contrary to popular belief, he did not declare his independence of the Mughal emperor. On the other hand, he acknowledged the latter's overlordship. In his testament recorded just before his death, he advised his son and successor always to be loyal to the Mughal emperor.[9]

The Three Successors (1748–62)

Though the first Nizam had nominated his son, Nasir Jung, as his successor, internecine warfare soon flared up. In the struggle for succession, Nasir Jung was killed in December 1750. His sister's son, Muzaffar Jung, succeeded him. He, in turn, was killed after a rule of barely six weeks. In 1751, his uncle, and Nasir Jung's brother, Salabat Jung, became the Nizam with the help of the French. Later, he switched over to the English and ruled till 1762. Soon thereafter, his brother, Nizam Ali Khan pushed him out and became the Nizam. In this tumultuous decade and a half, one-third of the territory held by the first Nizam was lost to the British, and by the time Nizam Ali Khan became the Nizam in 1762, he had become a protégé of theirs.

The three Nizams succeeding the first in fourteen years were not granted the title of Asaf Jah by the Mughal emperor. So, they are not counted in the Asaf Jahi dynasty.

The second Asaf Jah, Nizam Ali Khan, shifted the capital of the Deccan from Aurangabad to Hyderabad in 1763. In the war with Tipu Sultan of Mysore, in 1798–9, he sided with the British. When Tipu was defeated and killed in 1799, the Nizam got the districts of Cudappah and Khammam as his share of the booty.

It was during the period of Nizam II that the British entered into the Treaty of Subsidiary Alliance with the Nizam in 1798. The construction of the Residency building was taken up in the same year.

The British established the cantonment of the city of Secunderabad during the rule of the third Nizam, Sikander Jah (ruled 1803–29). It came to be called the twin city of Hyderabad.

The fourth Nizam, Nasir-ud-Dowla (ruled 1829–57), ceded Berar to the British in settlement of the arrears of Rs 64 lakh, and to defray the future expenses of the Hyderabad Contingent.

In the nineteenth century, it was common for people to keep firearms for their protection. Enugula Veeraswamy, a Brahmin from Chennai, passed through Hyderabad on his way to Varanasi for a pilgrimage in 1830–1. He records in his journal that 'every person in the city is armed and the milder ones were beaten up or cut down by these armed persons'.[10] He compared Hyderabad to Patna 'where people used their arms as ornaments'.[11]

General Fraser, who was Resident during 1838–52, estimated that 26,000 persons out of a population of 300,000 were armed—some to the teeth—and said that he could raise 75,000 armed men from the city without any difficulty. The law and order situation was therefore lax. The Arabs and Rohillas who commanded the irregular troops of 30,000 were a great menace.[12] Salar Jung I, the Prime Minister (1853–83), had to put them down with a combination of great tact and firmness.

In the Mutiny of 1857, Nizam V, Nasir-ud-Dowla (ruled 1857–69), under the advice of his Prime Minister, Salar Jung I, sided with the British and thus saved them. In gratitude, the British made generous presents to the Nizam, wrote off a debt of five million rupees and returned Raichur, Doab and Naldurg to him. In 1861, the new title of the Star of India was also conferred upon the Nizam.

After 1857, the British wanted to finish whatever was left of the symbols of the Mughal empire. Theoretically, the Nizam was still the viceroy of the Mughal emperor. The Emperor had been deported to Rangoon. The British, therefore, forced the Nizam to proclaim his independence of the Mughals by striking coins in his name and by having his name recited in the *khutba* (the Friday exordium)—two symbols of sovereignty in Islam. But the bond of subservience to the Mughal emperor was deeply ingrained in the Nizams. According to a story, when the seventh Nizam, Osman Ali Khan, visited the grave of Aurangzeb in Aurangabad in 1930, he wore the full uniform of the Governor subedar of the Deccan and the attendant at the grave recited his string of titles and announced to the grave that the subedar of the Deccan had come to pay his respects to the deceased emperor![13]

Mahboob Ali Khan was two-and-a-half years old when he became the sixth Nizam in 1869. The Resident took objection to his installation because prior permission of the Viceroy was taken for that. He was told that no permission was ever taken before and none was considered necessary. That indeed had been the position and the Resident had to accept it.

Until then, the Resident and his officials used to attend the Nizam's durbar bareheaded and barefooted. They used to sit on the floor along with the Indian nobles. Piqued by the incident, the Resident said that he would attend the durbar of the new Nizam without the headgear but wearing shoes. Also, he and his officers would sit on chairs and not on the floor. Willy-nilly, this demand had to be conceded. However, it would have been odd if the Indian nobles sat on the ground while the Resident and his entourage sat on chairs. An ingenious arrangement was therefore worked out. While chairs were put on one side, on the other side the level was raised by putting wooden *takhts*—planks—on which white sheets were spread. The accession of the toddling Nizam thus marked a departure in the old court etiquette, which subtly underlined the superior status of the British *vis-à-vis* the Indians.[14] This was to have long-term repercussions and set in motion changes in the dress and seating of the Indian nobles.

Hitherto, the Nizams used to undergo an oriental education, which included Arabic, Persian, Urdu, and the martial arts. For the child-Nizam, the British insisted on a liberal and sound education under the supervision of a British tutor. Mahboob was thus the first Nizam who could converse in English and wore European dress. He was a dandy and never wore the same dress twice. He had the largest wardrobe in the world—a hall 73 meters long in which two storeys of almirahs were neatly arranged.

Mahboob was a spendthrift, eccentric, and generous to a fault. He would frequently go incognito to the city at night to find out how people lived and what they thought of him. He was impulsive in his actions.

People believed that a mere touch by Nizam VI could cure a person of snakebite. Anybody could approach him at any time. Those who could not might just invoke his name. People still do that. His popularity was so great and universal that Hindus believed him to be the incarnation of Manik Prabhu, the saint of Humnabad. He died at the age of 45 in 1911.

The Last Nizam

His son, Mir Osman Ali Khan, succeeded him in 1911 at the age of 26. He was completely Anglicized and was known to enjoy Western wines and ballroom dancing.

Hyderabad was the largest Indian Princely State. Until the early twentieth century, Hyderabad remained a walled city with 14 gates and an equal number of *khidkis* (postern gates).

Osman Ali Khan was reputed to be the richest man of his time. He himself had no idea of his wealth. It was not surprising for a man whose privy purse was five million rupees, and whose personal estate yielded Rs 25 million a year. In 1919, he sold the six volumes of his poems for one guinea each (a guinea equalled twenty-one rupees).[15]

He was also presented *nazars* by whoever was granted the privilege of an audience. Two Nazar Durbars were held every year—on Eid, and on his birthday. All nobles, men of rank, and officers presented nazars to him there. The present of even one mango from his garden or a part of his dinner (*khasa*), sent to a subject randomly chosen, had to be acknowledged by presenting a nazar the next day. The minimum amount for a nazar was one gold coin and four silver—twenty-four rupees.

The man who had so much money lived an extremely frugal life. He wore the same cap for years—even when the ring of sweat and oil on its rim cried for its replacement. His clothes showed no sign of having been ironed. Numerous visitors to his residence testified to his cluttered, undusted drawing room. His jewels lay bundled up in all sorts of places from locked cellars to the floor underneath his bedstead.

Though parsimonious in his lifestyle, he made some significant contributions to the State. Parts of the old city destroyed by the floods of 1908 were built up on the blueprints prepared by the renowned engineer-statesman, Sir M. Visveswarayya. The river Musi was tamed. A scheme for providing protected water was completed. A wide concrete bazaar 'Patthar Gatti' was laid up to the Charminar. Mir Osman Ali Khan did not build any palaces. Instead, he undertook a number of public works. Some of the stately buildings—the Osmania University, the Osmania Hospital, the High Court, the State Central Library—rose to embellish the city skyline. With the decline of Lucknow, and later, of Rampur, Hyderabad remained the only Muslim state to patronize men of letters in Urdu and Persian. Poets and writers thus flocked to Hyderabad in search of fortune. Mushairas[16]—poetic gatherings—were held at the palaces of the nobles. The poets from other parts of India, awed and attracted by the beauty of the city, gave it the sobriquet of *uroos-ul-balad*—'bride amongst cities'. It became a centre of culture and rivalled Lucknow in the courtesy and politeness of its people.

During the Second World War, the Nizam helped the British liberally. For that he was given the title of His Exalted Highness. He was also allowed to use the title of Prince of Berar for his heir-apparent.

Political Awakening

The last Nizam saw the emergence of political demand for a popular, representative government. On the other hand, an attempt was made by a radical Muslim party, *Majlis-e-Ittehadul-Mussalmeen* (Council for the Union of Muslims) founded in 1927, to set up an Islamic state in Hyderabad. Two months before the Indian Independence in 1947, the Nizam declared his intention to become independent. After prolonged and unsuccessful negotiations, the Government of India launched 'Police Action' against Hyderabad on 13 September 1947. Four days later, it was integrated into India.

After the promulgation of the Constitution of India in 1950, elections were held in Hyderabad in 1952 and the Nizam was appointed its Raj Pramukh. In 1956, the States in India were reorganized on a linguistic basis. The old State of Hyderabad was trifurcated. Nine Telugu-speaking districts of Hyderabad were merged with Andhra to create the new state of Andhra Pradesh.

The Nizam asked to be relieved as the constitutional head of the new state. He retreated into his shell—the King Kothi.

His death in 1967 marked the end of an era. The Nizams did not build any mausoleums for themselves—or for their predecessors. Of the seven Nizams, five are buried in graves in a gallery in the compound of the Mecca Mosque. The first Nizam was buried in Khuldabad and the last by the side of his mother and infant son in the compound of the Judi Mosque close to his residence, the King Kothi.

Social and Cultural Life of Hyderabad

Hyderabad has been renowned for what has been called its 'composite' culture. It is a way of life with a flavour not noticed anywhere else in India. It is a product of many factors, especially its geography and history.

The location of Hyderabad in the centre of India has placed it crucially on the highways from the north to the south and from the east to the west. Its equable climate has been another attraction all through the ages.

Historically, Hyderabad was part of the Hindu kingdom of Kakatiya (1000–1321). The Sultan of Delhi, Alauddin Khilji reduced it to a vassal state in 1310. Mohammad Tughlaq annexed it in 1321 and it remained a part of the Delhi Sultanate till 1347. In that year, a group of local chiefs revolted against Tughlaq and set up the Bahmani Sultanate. In 1518, Sultan Quli who was Governor of Golconda, of which Hyderabad was a part, broke away from the Bahmanis and founded the Qutb Shahi dynasty, which lasted till 1687.

Up in the north, Mahmud of Ghazni annexed Punjab in 1020 and stationed his Persian-speaking army there. Muhammad Ghori dislodged him in 1186. During this long period of 166 years of interaction between the language of the army, Persian, and the local language, Punjabi, a new language was born. It underwent further development in Delhi and imbibed the influences of languages and dialects spoken in and around Delhi after Ghori's general, Qutubuddin Aibak, subjugated Delhi in 1193. Till the end of the seventeenth century, it was called Hindi, or Hindwi. It was that language which first the army of Alauddin Khilji brought to the south when he completed the conquest of the south in 1310. This was accentuated when in 1327, Muhammed Tughlaq shifted the capital of India from Delhi to Deogri, rechristened by him as Daulatabad. The Bahmanis followed a policy of isolation from the north. The language thus had no interaction with the languages of the north, but was influenced mainly by Gujarati and Marathi, and to a lesser extent by Kannada, and Telugu. That language came to be called Dakhni. It had a base of Punjabi with an interlacing of other southern languages.[17] It is considered by many scholars to be the original Urdu, or as Professor Masud Husain Khan calls it, 'Proto-Urdu'.[18] It was distinctly different from the northern Urdu and in spite of the integration of Hyderabad with the Mughal Delhi in 1687, retained its distinct identity.

Thus by the time the city of Bhagnagar (now Hyderabad) was founded in 1591, it had acquired layers of religious and linguistic influences from many sources. The strongest of them was the Iranian influence, since like the Iranians, the Qutb Shahi rulers professed the Shia sect of Islam. They also acknowledged the Shah of Iran as their overlord. That influence has persisted and today persons of Iranian origin in Hyderabad number about 5000. Most of them have become Indian citizens. Next to Mumbai, the largest number of Iranians lives in Hyderabad—over 400. It was in recognition of that fact that an Iranian Consulate General was established in Hyderabad in 1970. The Irani cafés strewn all over the city are the favourite resorts of the common man, including the impecunious poets.

While earlier, there were only influences, the architecture of the new city was Islamic in concept. The German architect, Jan Pieper, has shown with reference to the chapter and verse of the Quran, how, in accordance with the decree of the founder, Mohammad Quli, Hyderabad was built as a replica of the mythical Islamic heaven.[19] We have the testimony of many foreign visitors and chroniclers, like Tavernier, Thevenot, Methwold, and the Abbé Carré, to mention only a few, that Hyderabad was a very flourishing commercial centre in the seventeenth century. Abbé Carré's observation in 1673 is typical:

It is a very spacious town, situated in a flat country, watered by a fine river. It is full of strangers and merchants, and trade is carried on by foreigners and others without any or particular business. There is such a concourse of every kind of people, merchandise and riches, that the place seems to be the centre of all trade in the East.[20]

Niccolao Manucci, an adventurer, who was in Hyderabad in 1678, refers to many Christians who were in the service of the Sultan of Golconda. He secured the job of the Sultan's French physician who had died. Also, he was able to escape from Golconda due to the influence of the Dutch envoy and the Father Vicar of Golconda.[21]

Thus, right from the beginning, Hyderabad was a cosmopolitan city. During the Qutb Shahi period (1518–1687), its rulers owed their allegiance to the king of Persia. The language of the court was Persian. There was a deep influence of Iran on every aspect of life in Hyderabad. When it became a part of the Deccan *Suba* of the Mughals, an overlay of Mughal influence came to manifest itself in architecture, dress, food, and manners.

Architecture

Most of the Qutb Shahi palaces and buildings were destroyed by the Mughal invasion in 1687. The Asaf Jahis therefore started on a spree of their own construction. In their architecture, one finds a mix of neo-Qutb Shahi, European, Mughal, and Rajasthani styles.

Salabat Jung (1751–62) built the core of the Chow Mahalla Palace complex. The four main palaces comprising the complex are: the Afzal Mahal, the Mahtab Mahal, the Tahniyat Mahal, and the Aftab Mahal. Of these, Afzal Mahal is the most imposing, a two-storeyed building with a European façade of Corinthian columns and a parapet without pediment. All the four buildings are laid around a large courtyard garden with a marble cistern at the centre.

The second Nizam constructed the Purani Haveli located towards the north-east of the Charminar in 1777 for his son, Sikander Jah. The Purani Haveli complex is U-shaped with a single-storeyed central building in European style flanked by two double-storeyed oblong wings (nearly 300 metres) of which the western one has the famous wooden wardrobe—reputedly the longest in the world. Purani Haveli is one of the most important architectural landmarks of Hyderabad combining European façades with traditional Indian courtyards. The complex also includes two annexes attached to the northern ends of the parallel wings.

The sixth Nizam, Mehboob, himself built a number of palaces and acquired some. The Saifabad Palace, built in 1887, was never occupied and was used as the State Secretariat. At the time of writing this, it is under demolition. He also built the Mehboob Mansion on the outskirts of Hyderabad in the late nineteenth century. It was a large palace built in a combination of classical European and Mughal style.

Nobles' Palaces

In the hierarchy of nobles of Hyderabad, the Paigah family ranked immediately next to the ruling family of the Nizams. The Paigah were also the foremost palace builders of Hyderabad. The Falaknuma Palace is located on top of a hill about four kilometers south of the Charminar. It was built by the Paigah noble, Nawab Vicar-ul-Umra, who later became Prime Minister of Hyderabad (1894–1901). The main palace was designed by English architects and completed in 1892. The sixth Nizam acquired it in 1895 and occasionally lived here. He died in this building in 1911.

It is one of the largest and most important palaces of India. The interior of the main building has a marble entrance hall and fountain, and Italian marble staircase supporting marble figures, lined with portraits of British Governors General. The reception room is in Louis XIV style. Elsewhere there are French tapestries, beautiful inlaid furniture from Kashmir, and Victorian artifacts.

The Nizam used the Palace as his guest house for dignitaries. No one lower in rank than the Governor General of India was accommodated here.

Vicar-ul-Umra's palace in Begumpet built in the 1880s is a large two-storeyed neo-classical building with a portico, semicircular arches, unfluted Corinthian columns, projected and pedimented windows, and deep-arcaded verandahs on all four sides.

The most important palace of the Paigah Bashir-ud-Dowla, the Bashir Bagh Palace, has been demolished. Asman Garh, a smaller but interesting European-style palace on a hilltop in Dilsukh Nagar, still survives.

The Malwala Palace, built by the leading Kayasth family of Hyderabad in 1847, was located along the road leading towards the east from the Charminar. It was one of the few wooden palaces of Hyderabad built in the late Mughal and Rajasthani style.

Raja Dhanrajgirji, who belonged to a family of nineteenth-century religious preceptors and bankers, built the Gyan Bagh Palace. It is one of the best buildings of Hyderabad in European style and is the best preserved.

Nawab Fakhr-ul-Mulk, a high-ranking noble, built the Irum Manzil Palace at Panjagutta. It is a vast complex in European style with an ornate baroque façade, occupying a commanding position on a hillock. Now it houses the offices of the Public Works Department.

The nobles of Hyderabad decided to present a palace to the sixth Nizam on his fortieth birthday. According to his wishes, it was built in the Rajasthan style of architecture. By the time the building was ready, the Nizam had died. Now it houses the State Assembly.[22]

In the Public Garden, there are a number of outstanding buildings like the State Archaeological Museum, the Moti Masjid, and the Silver Jubilee Complex built to commemorate the Silver Jubilee of the sixth Nizam in 1937.

As mentioned above, the last Nizam, Mir Osman Ali Khan (1911–48), did not build any palace for himself. He came to fancy one in the new city and bought it from one Kamal Khan. However, he built a number of impressive public buildings. Some of them came up as a part of the renewal of the city after the Great Flood of the Musi devastated the city in 1908. The most prominent amongst them, the building of the Arts College of the Osmania University, incorporates the dominant elements of the Hindu with the Saracenic styles of architecture.[23]

Dress

In Hyderabad, boys wore *kurta pajama*, jacket, and *topis* (caps) of different kinds, like the Mushadzadi topi, Roomi topi, round topi, and Dupalli topi.

Men wore kurta pajama at home, and *sherwani* outside. Sherwani is the Hyderabadi counterpart of the *achkan* (high close-collar buttoned-up long coat) of the north. The sherwani differed from the achkan in three respects: Its collar was higher, it was loose, and it went below the knees in length. It also had pocket covers like the English jacket. It was made not only in white and black, but also on different type of colours including *kalamkari* and cloth-of-gold. Later, sherwanis were also made of tweed for use in winter. The pajama worn in Hyderabad was a notch higher than the ankles. The footwear generally matched the colour of the sherwani.

On the sherwani, a belt called *bugloos* was worn. Val Prinsep, who visited Hyderabad in the course of his visit to India to make a painting for Queen Victoria on her being proclaimed the Empress of India in 1878, believed that the term 'bugloos' came from the English term 'buckles'.[24] The *dastar* was raised and somewhat pointed in the middle. Different nobles had their own slight variation in the style and colour. One could not go to the court without the formal dress of dastar and bugloos. Even Sir Sayyed Ahmed Khan was not allowed to meet Nizam VI because he did not wear that dress. Towards the end of the nineteenth century, the Turkish cap—*Fez*—became popular amongst the common people.

Women had an elaborate range of outfits—*dupatta* (head scarf), *peshwaz*, *lehenga*, and sarees.

A girl always started with wearing kurta pajama, which was different from that of the boys. They were made mostly of mashroo—satin silk with stripes or dots. For special occasions, the pajamas would be made of Benares brocade. Girls also wore topis made of Benares tissues with heavy gold work for occasions. When a girl reached puberty, she would start wearing a small dupatta two metres in length and gradually start wearing a *khada dupatta* of six metres. At the time of her wedding, a girl was given her first *kurti*—cloth to be worn with khada dupatta. Kurti is a sleeveless kurta with a round deep neckline made of sheer fabric—mostly from *karga,* fine cotton net intricately embroidered with gold thread—and is very heavy to wear. The entire outfit had to be made in contrasting colours.

Sarees were mostly worn by grown-up women. Hindu women wore sarees with blouses or *cholis*, or *sadri choli*. Muslim women wore sarees with either a *kurti choli* or kurta. Only married women wore kurti choli.[25]

Cuisine

The Asaf Jahs were gourmets. Their fondness for the good life raised their cuisine to the level of an art.

The south is a rice-eating region. A liberal dose of chillies is mixed with the rice. The waves of Muslim invaders added meat of all types to the rice. There was literally no part of the body of various animals that did not become part of a special dish. The result was a cuisine rich in variety and delicious in taste.

Colonel Mohsin Beg, a migrant from Hyderabad to Pakistan, refers nostalgically to the 200 items in a menu listed by Nasiruddin Hashmi. He himself has prepared a list of 112 items of main dishes, 76 types of sweet dishes, and 33 types of chutneys and *achars*. Amongst the well-known typical dishes are *Bagahare Baingan, Tihari, Chakhna, Dalcha, Sukhmukh Salam Bakre ka Dam Pukht, Jheenge, Shikampur, Tootak, Tamate ka Cut, Mirch ka Salan, Harees, Biryani, and Keema* in various forms.

Amongst the sweet dishes are *Puran Poori, Double ka Meetha, Khobani ka Meetha, Gosht ka Meetha, Warqi Khajoor, Sheer Khurma, Ande ka Halwa, Badam ki Jali, and Nimish.*[26]

Every noble's house had its own specialty. One of Muazzam Jah's dinners is described in the book later. Food was generally eaten on a low table for eight, called *chowki*. The diners sat on the ground on dhurries covered by white sheets. Bolsters were provided for supporting the back.

Maharaja Kishen Pershad who was twice Prime Minister of Hyderabad was himself such a good cook that he claimed to have cooked for an entire month without repeating a single dish.[27] Once when Nawab Zafar Jung invited the Paigah noble, Khurshid Jah, to honour him by tasting his chutneys, he took him at his word and said he would accept his invitation provided only chutneys and bread were served. The host provided more than 100 types of chutneys![28]

Nawab Sarvar-ul-Mulk, the grandson of the renowned Urdu poet, Mirza Ghalib, who came from Delhi and became tutor, and later Private Secretary, to the sixth Nizam, observed that on special occasions 'people cooked a special dish which they called "Biryanee" (rice, meat and spices, cooked together). And in truth, no better dish is cooked anywhere in India'.[29]

Another factor which gave the culture of Hyderabad a special flavour was that for over six centuries, from 1321 to 1948, it had uninterrupted Muslim rule and a vast Hindu subject population. That juxtaposition necessitated a discreet accommodation on both sides and gave rise to a rare synthesis.

Language

The earlier interaction between various Indian linguistic and other groups was followed, in the seventeenth century, by the interface with the European powers, particularly the French and the British. By 1763, the influence of the French had waned. In 1798, by the Treaty of Subsidiary Alliance, Hyderabad became a vassal state of the British. The Resident, Kirkpatrick built a magnificent mansion as his official residence.[30] There he installed his Muslim wife, Khairunissa. The Nizam gave him the title of Hashmat Jung. The Residency became a source of radiating European influence on a medieval Indian city. It is interesting to note that right until the end of the premiership of Salar Jung I (1853–83), all but 28 officials of Hyderabad were forbidden to meet the Resident and his officials. After his death, the restrictions were relaxed, and the young Nizam VI himself started not only wearing Western dress, but also accepting the Resident's hospitality. The nobility started visiting England and sending their children abroad for education.

The majority of the people of Hyderabad spoke Telugu. Other languages spoken were Marathi, Kannada, and Urdu. However, Urdu was the official language. So, people spoke their mother tongue at home and Urdu outside. The more sophisticated upper classes and those who were ambitious added English to their repertoire. 'By the 1820s, a European social life had begun developing in Hyderabad, as the power and the numbers of English personnel increased steadily.'[31] The recruitment of a large number of Muslims from British India, and particularly from the north to high and crucial administrative jobs also had a salutary effect on the prevailing social and cultural climate of the city. The orientation of the newcomers was different and they started settling down outside the walled city near the Residency. At the close of the nineteenth century, 'a vigorous and eclectic Hyderabadi society seemed to be developing in which all men of wealth and standing could participate'.[32]

The assimilation of the English with the higher levels of society was so much that on 17 February 1890, the Prime Minister, Sir Asman Jah, threw a fancy dress party in his palace at Bashir Bagh. About 200 men and women attended the party. Of them, a good number were English couples. One English woman came as a *nautch* girl dancing to the tune of the *duff* beaten by her husband. They drank and danced. Some sat and watched the *mujra* and threw coins at the dancing girl in Indian clothes. The sit-down dinner had eleven courses with a choice of continental and *Mughlai* dishes. Amongst the five desserts, the most popular was *nimish*. It is the fluff of boiled milk mixed with sugar and enriched by dew. This had been added by keeping it under the open sky overnight.[33]

Religious Harmony

Generally, there was greater religious harmony amongst the people in the south than in the north. For one, the much-hated *jiziya* (poll-tax) was never imposed on non-Muslims in the south. In addition, there were positive cases of shows of liberality on the part of the Muslim rulers. Mohammed Quli, the founder of Hyderabad bequeathed to the city its pervasive and abiding spirit of mutual harmony. In his poetry, he denounced the differentiation between temple and mosque. He celebrated Hindu festivals like Holi and referred to God not as Allah, or *Khuda*, but by the Hindu appellations of *Kartar, Dayawant,* and *Dayawan*.[34] The last Qutb Shahi ruler, Tana Shah, refused to dismiss his Hindu Prime Minister, Madanna, which had been one of the demands of Aurangzeb.

There is one instance of the third Nizam exhibiting unusual liberality in his outlook. The Kayasths had accompanied the first Nizam from the north to the Deccan as his record-keepers. In 1803, one of them, Raja Bhavani Pershad, built the first Kayasth temple at Rambagh in a village near Attapur. When the temple was ready, the Nizam performed the ceremony of the installation of the idols of Rama, Sita, and Lakshmana. He also granted a jagir of 12,000 rupees for its maintenance. Thus, the 'idol worshipper' and the 'idol breaker' came together in a touching gesture.[35]

There are other examples of temples and *jathras* (pilgrimages and religious processions) which enjoyed support from the State. The jathra to the temple of Balaji near Saroor Nagar started in 1826 and was financed by the treasury of the Peshkar—the highest functionary after the Diwan. The temple of Lord Krishna on the way to the Rambagh was provided a *jagir* for its maintenance. The Sita Ram Bagh temple built by Mahajan Seth Puranmal was similarly provided.

Raja Ishwari Pershad, a noble of Hyderabad, had started a celebration of *Lila* on *Janamashtami* (birthday of Lord Krishna) in his house when he was at Aurangabad. He continued the tradition when he shifted to Hyderabad in 1859. Salar Jung I made an annual grant of five hundred rupees for it. It was confirmed by Nawab Vicar-ul-Umra in 1904.[36]

The great flood of 1908 in the Musi river was the worst in recorded history. It destroyed or damaged about 19,000 houses, and claimed 15,000 lives. The old people of Hyderabad refer to it even today as *Parson ki Tughyani*—the flood of day-before-yesterday!

The sixth Nizam, Mir Mahboob Ali Khan, was told that the flood occurred because the goddess Bhavani was in anger and she had to be appeased. He carried a silver plate with five earthen lamps and a saree on his head and performed *arti* of the goddess. People believed that the floods started receding after that.[37]

Sagar Mal, a Kayasth, came with the first Nizam to Hyderabad. He was appointed the head of the *Daftar-e-Mal* (Revenue Record Office) in 1761. This office later became hereditary and the family came to be known as Malwala. In due course, it acquired great power and a lot of property in the heart of the city. Its residence came to be called the Malwala Palace. It became the head of the Mathur caste of the Kayasth clan. All the Mathurs gathered at the Malwala Palace on every Dussehra, a festival celebrated to mark the defeat of Ravana by Rama. There they performed '*dwat puja*'— worship of their traditional tools, namely the inkpot and pen. The Malwala Palace was illuminated on the birthday of Prophet Muhammad and alms were given away on that occasion, as also on the annual commemoration ceremony of Abdul Qadir Gilani, the founder of the Sufi Qadri order in India. During Muharram, the family displayed its *taziya* and set up a shelter to offer water to the processionists.[38]

There is the case of Akbar Yar Jung Bahadur, a judge, and later Home Secretary. He was invited by the Young Men's Kayasth Union as the chief guest to the *Janamashtami* function on 11 August 1936. In his speech he termed Lord Krishna as the Prophet of India and invoked the benediction reserved by Muslims only for their acknowledged prophets: 'May peace be upon him.' That earned him the wrath of the conservative sections of Muslims who brayed for his blood. But he escaped with a mere reprimand from the Nizam to refrain from making public speeches on controversial subjects.[39]

The Christians also enjoyed a certain measure of patronage from the Nizams. We have noted above that a Catholic Church existed in the fort city of Golconda during the Qutb Shahi period. St Joseph Church was established in 1870.

The Protestants established the St George's Church in 1867. The Grammar School started in its compound still exists. The Nizam gave a grant of 6000 rupees to this church.

The Missionary Society was started by Goldsmith in 1891 near the Residency.[40]

Another interesting pointer to this happy mix of communities is the story of a French soldier of fortune. Monsieur Raymond became the commander of the forces of the second Nizam. By 1795, he had established a formidable army of 15,000 men and even set up a foundry for the manufacture of artillery. He died suddenly in 1798 at the age of 43. His popularity amongst his men was so great that his Muslim followers corrupted his name into Musa Rahim, while Hindus gave him the name of Musa Ram. An annual *urs* used to be held till about 50 years ago in his memory. A locality called Musa Ram Bagh is still prospering.

Thus, a general climate of religious harmony prevailed. It came under a strain only after the emergence of the *Anjuman-e-Ittehad-e-Musalmeen* in 1927, and particularly in the two years 1946–8 preceding the integration of Hyderabad with India when the *razakars*—the armed wing of the *Majlis*—made a bid for power to establish an Islamic state in Hyderabad. Even in those dark days, there are examples of Muslims who protested against the attitude of their co-religionists and risked a lot. Shoeb Ullah Khan, the journalist, lost his life. Qazi Abdul Ghaffar resigned as Director of Public Relations and left Hyderabad. Fareed Mirza and Mehdi Ali suffered in their official career in the civil service. Nawab Akbar Ali Khan took a daring stand on the issue in his public life.

The contribution of a small community, the Parsis, cannot be overlooked in this account. The first Parsi who came to Hyderabad was Mulla Kavus bin Rustam Jalal. Arriving there in 1711, he stayed as an honoured companion of the second Nizam till his death in 1802. In 1830, Raja Chandulal, the Prime Minister, specifically invited them to open banking firms in Hyderabad. Within two years, the firm of Pestonji Vikaji became the principal banking house in Hyderabad. They loaned money to the Government, and in return, the revenues of Berar and Aurangabad were mortgaged to them. Their prosperity and influence was such that they were allowed to retain a small armed force and the mint at Aurangabad was entrusted to them.[41] Salar Jung I, the Prime Minister of Hyderabad (1853–83), in his efforts to modernize the medieval administration of Hyderabad, recruited men of ability from different parts of India. Amongst them were a small number of Parsis. Their advantage was that they knew both English and Persian well. They also kept aloof from politics and court intrigues. According to Eckehard Kulke, 'This is the reason for the numerically relatively large Parsi community in Hyderabad that was called into the State under Salar Jung to reform the administration'.[42] The Parsis were found in all departments of the government. Some of them rose to the highest offices. One, Pestonji Bapooji Chenoy, became the first India Master of the Mint at Hyderabad. Faridoonji rose to be the Prime Minister of the State in 1922 and as Nawab Faridoon-ul-Mulk Bahadur, served in that capacity for about two years. The last Parsi to wield enormous influence was Cooveji Taraporevala who was a financial wizard. As Financial Adviser to Nizam VII, he was responsible for the numerous Trusts created by the last Nizam to take care of many matters including the smallest needs of his survivors.

Art and Entertainment

Another area that exhibited the diversity of influences was that of the performing arts. To the original Carnatic music and the Kuchipudi and Bharat Natyam dance forms popular in the south, the Muslim rulers introduced both secular and spiritual music from Arabia and Persia which had already been established in the north of India. We find frequent mention of the classical ragas of Hindustani music in the poetry of Mohammad Quli Qutb Shah. Sultan Ali Adil Shah II of Bijapur (1571–1627) wrote a book *Kitaab-e-Nauras* comprising 59 *geets* (songs). This showed his knowledge of the Indian tradition of aesthetics first enunciated in the *Natya Sastra* of Bharata.

The Asaf Jahis had a department of *Arbaab-e-Nishaat*, which today would translate as the department of culture and entertainment. Raja Bhavani Pershad who constructed the first Kayasth Temple referred to above was the head of that department. On the annual Ram Navami celebrations at the Ram Bagh temple, a procession was taken out in which 300 dancing girls and musicians participated. 'For three days following Rama's birthday, Hindustani classical vocal music concerts lasted the entire night and leading nobles including Muslims comprised the audience.'[43] Mah Laqa Bai Chanda was a favourite courtesan of Nizam II and later of Mir Alam and Chandulal. She is reputed to be the first woman-poet of Urdu in India whose poetry was published. The later Nizams continued the tradition of keeping cultured courtesans well-versed in music. The nobles too patronized music and musicians. Once, in the early twentieth century, when arrangements were being made for a private soirée by the staff of Nizam VI, Pandit Moti Ram, father of the celebrated classical singer Pandit Jasraj, suggested that the Nizam should be seated on the floor. The officials thought it was scandalous to make such a suggestion, and said that His Highness would sit on a gilded chair. Pandit Moti Ram muttered mischievously, 'You wait and see.' The Nizam came and sat on his chair in front of the maestro. The singer then started singing raga Yaman with the wording:

> *Aane naa doongi laaj Ali par*
> *Hasan Husain par waari jaaoon*
>
> I shall not let Ali be embarrassed
> I shall die for Hasan and Husain.

Ali was the son-in-law of the Prophet, and Hasan and Husain were his sons. They were all assassinated and Muslims revere them. So, when their names were recited in the song, out of deference the Nizam got down from his chair and sat on the floor.[44]

The last Nizam invited musicians like Bade Ghulam Ali Khan, Fayaz Khan, Hirabai Barodkar, Saraswati Rane, Suresh Baboo, D.V. Paluskar, and others.[45] Pandit Jasraj's father, Pandit Moti Ram, used to sing before the sixth Nizam. The Deccan Radio also played a role in bringing together the music of the south and north.

A better knowledge of English, combined with more interaction with the Residency and other Europeans, and the return of Hyderabad nobles after their education abroad, resulted in Western music beginning to make an impact on the élite of Hyderabad. The seventh Nizam himself was fond of ballroom dancing in his early years. Thus, 'a few music schools sprang up in Secunderabad and dozens of pianos were imported in the twin cities .... Anglo-Indians and Christians of comparatively humbler means also sustained the interest. Choral singing in churches was also cultivated and this continues on a large scale even today. Christmas and Easter Sundays continue to be big events for those interested in such music.'[46]

By the beginning of the rule of Nizam VII in 1911, the base of the Mughlai way of life had been given a patina of Western culture. But its distinct identity in relation to dress, cuisine, language and manners, as well as architecture remained.

The politeness of manners compares favourably with that of Lucknow. It seemed that people were forever *salaam*ing each other. 'Thank You' was not only uttered, but was expressed through repeated *salaam*s. The young met elders with bowed heads, which they literally shoved into the belly of elders. One can still encounter it in old families. It is called *pet mein mundi daalnaa*—'putting head into the tummy'. It makes it easy for the elder one to pat the head of the younger one by way of blessing.

The resultant culture was proudly proclaimed by the people of Hyderabad as *Ganga-Jamani* in Urdu and 'composite' in English. It had acquired such a distinctive identity that Sarojini Naidu in a letter to Jawaharlal Nehru on 11 May 1925 said proudly, 'I wish you could share the delight—the real delight of being in Hyderabad boating on the Mir Alam, of lounging and loafing around and meeting the most truly cosmopolitan society in India, which needless to say haunts the Golden Threshold [the name of her residence] even unto four generations beginning with the generation that was my parents—almost prehistoric!'[47]

The fact that Hyderabad stood out in its special appeal is borne out by the observation of Philip Mason of the India Civil Service (ICS), and the author of 'Men Who Ruled India' as late as 1947. When India became independent, he took premature retirement from the ICS. On his way home he was invited by Princess Durreshahwar, wife of the Prince of Berar to pass through Hyderabad to help set up some sort of 'school' for the education of her two sons. During his stay, he attended a birthday party:

'Who is that little boy?' I asked my nearest neighbour and she told me a name I have forgotten, but unmistakably Hindu, some Ram Swarup or Jag Deo. 'But he is wearing a Muslim hat!'

'Oh, here in Hyderabad we do not care for things like that', his neighbour explained gaily, 'it is one of the nice things that we are so delightfully cosmopolitan'.[48]

A year later, after the Police Action, the Military Governor of Hyderabad, General J.N. choudhury, was screening the senior officials of Hyderabad. They were all seated in a hall and his ADC, Captain Pyare Lal, called them up one by one for the interview. When he announced the name of Rai Janaki Pershad, he saw a dignified Muslim get up. 'Not you, yet. Please wait', said the ADC, and again called for Janaki Pershad. The same gentleman heaved himself up again. 'Not you, Mister', the ADC said in exasperation, 'I am calling Mr Rai Janaki Pershad.'

'Well, I am Janaki Pershad,' the officer replied with calm assertion. 'Then why are you dressed like a Muslim?' asked the captain in surprise.

'That is how we dress here,' replied Janaki Pershad.[49]

A tumultuous churning took place when the old State of Hyderabad was trifurcated and the largest chunk of nine of the sixteen districts was joined to the old Andhra State to form the new state of Andhra Pradesh in 1956. While many civil servants of the old State were transferred to Karnataka and Maharashtra, there was a large influx of officials from Andhra. This was followed by a rush of people from business and other classes. All those who used to go earlier to Madras for a good time found Hyderabad better in many respects. Amongst other things, unlike in Madras (now Chennai), there was no prohibition in the new capital. The population of the city began to increase at a very high rate.

Hyderabad is not a city, but a procession of cities. One sees many tableaux in that procession. Each has its own motif. Each gives a different picture. But they have so harmoniously coalesced that one sees a charming collage so different from what one comes across in other places in the country.

Nizam VII had a number of wives and concubines and sired twenty-five sons. Only two of them, from his principal wife, Dulhan Pasha, enjoyed an official position. The elder son was Mir Himayat Ali Khan, formally known as Azam Jah. He was born in February 1907. Since 1936, he carried the title of Prince of Berar though ironically Berar had ceased to be a part of Hyderabad in 1853. He was also the honorary commander-in-chief of the state forces. His official residence was the 'Bella Vista' Palace. It now houses the Administrative Staff College of India.

His younger brother, Mir Shujat Ali Khan, formally known as Muazzam Jah, was born nine months after his elder brother, in November 1907. He was called the Junior Prince and was the chairman of the City Improvement Board, which was established in 1912 to repair the damage caused by the Great Flood of 1908. He was fond of poetry and was himself a poet sporting the pen name *Shajee* (a variation on his real name and meaning 'the brave one'). He stayed in the Hill Fort Palace at the foot of Naubat Pahad, commanding a grand view of the Hussain Sagar Lake. The building was later leased out to the Ritz Hotel and is now lying vacant. It was built by Sir Nizamat Jung, and has its own story. Born in 1875, Jung served as Home Secretary, judge of the High Court, and member of the Executive Council of the Nizam. He retired in 1929. He had been educated at Cambridge and when he built the Hill Fort in 1923, he had in mind the castles of England and the style of architecture of the colleges of Cambridge University. But the building turned out to be too cumbersome for the bachelor scholar-administrator to manage. It was later purchased by the Nizam, expanded, and given to the Junior Prince as his official residence.

The marriage of the two princes was solemnized on the same day, on 12 November 1931 at Nice in France. The Prince of Berar was married to the only child of Abdul Majid, the last Sultan of Turkey and last Caliph of Islam who had been deposed by Kemal Ataturk in 1924. His bride, Princess Durreshahwar (literally, the 'great pearl'), was a tall and stately young woman of about eighteen. The Junior Prince was married to Niloufer (meaning lotus), a first cousin of Durreshahwar. She was about two years younger than her cousin and was a beauty.

Incidentally, the Nizam did not go for the wedding. Nor did any member of the immediate family. Only some members of the family of the ex-Sultan at Nice, some Turkish nobles, and a few friends attended the wedding on the side of the brides. The members of the Hyderabad delegation to the Round Table Conference in London constituted the groom's marriage party. They were Sir Hyder Nawaz Jung (later Sir Akbar Hydari, Prime Minister of Hyderabad), Sir Richard Trench, and Nawab Mehdi Yar Jung. The ex-Caliph himself conducted the religious ceremony. A holiday was declared in Hyderabad in celebration of the wedding.

The twin weddings were the melding of the Mughlai and the European cultures. The two Princesses by their example, encouraged the emergence of women into the open. In any case, purdah was not observed in the upper classes of women in Hyderabad.

The two Princesses were thoroughly westernized and were fond of outdoor life. While they adapted themselves to sarees, they did not observe any purdah and with their grace and charming manners, infused new life into Hyderabadi society. However, the two different ways of life could not be harmonized. The marriages therefore were not successful. Princess Durreshahwar went away to England with her two sons. Now close to ninety, she visits Hyderabad occasionally. Niloufer did not bear any children. Her husband, Muazzam Jah, developed a relationship with a woman, Razia Begum, who was married to a little-known poet. She bore him two daughters.

After some years of failed marriage, Niloufer went away to Paris. In spite of the reported entreaties of her husband and Ali Pasha, the son-in-law of

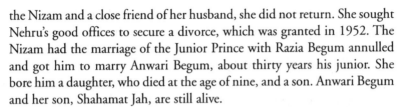

the Nizam and a close friend of her husband, she did not return. She sought Nehru's good offices to secure a divorce, which was granted in 1952. The Nizam had the marriage of the Junior Prince with Razia Begum annulled and got him to marry Anwari Begum, about thirty years his junior. She bore him a daughter, who died at the age of nine, and a son. Anwari Begum and her son, Shahamat Jah, are still alive.

In October 1949, the Nizam set up a trust of Rs 3 million each for Princess Shahwar and Niloufer. The latter settled down in Paris. In 1962 when she was about forty-seven, Niloufer married an American, Edward C. Pope. He was a former U.S. army officer and a film producer. It was a very happy marriage. Niloufer passed away in Paris in 1986. Before her death, she donated US$ 1000 for the Children's Hospital in Hyderabad, which is named after her. Her portrait adorns the entrance to the hospital. Edward Pope proposed to organize an exhibition of her wardrobe in Hyderabad, but it did not materialize.

The two Princes lived a sybaritic life. They were temperamentally different and were jealous of each other—a common feature in ruling houses. They held their own 'courts', moved in different orbits, and had separate sets of hangers-on. Poets, singers, and dancers surrounded the Junior Prince at night. He slept through the day dosed with sleeping pills.

While researching my book *Memoirs of a City*, I came across a book in Urdu entitled: *Darbaar-e-Dürbaar*. It literally means a 'Court of Pearls' or a 'Magnificent Court'. A number of poets were attached to the 'court' of the Junior Prince. Some of them were paid while others were honorary. They drank and ate with him and spent the whole night in gatherings where the Prince's poetic composition was sung about and praised. *Mujras*—dances by courtesans accompanied by singing—also took place.

According to tradition, a Muslim ruler should not only be a good soldier but also a penman—preferably a poet. *Sahib-e-saif-o-qalam* (master of sword and pen) is the ideal which Muslim rulers have always aspired to. The first two Nizams were poets in Persian. The last two Nizams composed poetry both in Persian and in Urdu. An anthology of the last Nizam was published by the Nizam's Trust posthumously. The rulers accorded poets much esteem and the height of ambition of every poet was to become the *ustad*—royal poetic preceptor of the ruler. Nawab Mirza 'Dagh',[50] the celebrated poet of Urdu, held such a position with the sixth Nizam. Jaleel Manakpuri[51] followed him in 1911 and continued in that position even with the seventh Nizam until his death in 1946. The poems of the last Nizam, along with the 'corrections' of the ustad in pencil, were published on the front page of the newspaper to which they were sent. The corrections were generally exclamations of praise and sometimes suggested, timorously and extremely respectfully, alternative wording.

Urdu poets were attracted to the courts of Muslim rulers of most Indian states. While they could earn good money and live a life of ease, it was a matter of prestige for the ruler to patronize the best talent. After the collapse of Avadh (Lucknow) and later of Rampur, Hyderabad became the last haven for Urdu poets. A good many of them came and tried their luck at Hyderabad. Dagh, Jaleel, Fani Badayuni, Bazm Afandi, Najm Afandi, Josh Maleehabadi, Jigar Muradabadi, Mahirul Qadri and many others prospered there. An additional reason for this influx was that Maharaja Kishen Pershad who was Prime Minister of Hyderabad for two spells lasting twenty-three years (1900–12 and 1925–36) was himself a poet and a great patron of men of letters. One poet brought another, pushed out somebody else, and so there were numerous groups and cliques of poets and writers.

Sidq Jaisi

One such poet was Sidq Jaisi. His real name was Mirza Tassaduq Hussain. He was born in Jais, in Bareilly district of Uttar Pradesh (then United Provinces). He first came to Hyderabad in 1923 in search of fortune and stayed with the poetic ustad of the sixth Nizam, Nawab Fasahat Jung 'Jaleel' Manakpuri, for eight months. He was aspiring for a professorship in Osmania University but was not qualified for it. Further, he did not possess a certificate of domicile in Hyderabad (called *mulki* certificate), which was a necessary requirement for getting a job in Hyderabad.

By the time he secured the certificate, a plague had broken out in the city and he went back to his native place. He returned after four years. By this time, Maharaja Kishen Pershad, after thirteen years in wilderness, had once again become the Prime Minister of Hyderabad. Sidq impressed the Maharaja with his poetry but did not get any benefit. Thereupon, in one gathering, he taunted him respectfully in a poem for not providing for him. Because of that, he was appointed as a teacher in the city Government High School. Later, he was transferred to Aurangabad, from where he retired in due course.

While in Hyderabad, he came to the notice of the Junior Prince through the good offices of the poet Fani and was made honorary courtier. Starting in 1931, Sidq spent seven years as an honorary courtier of the Prince. He thus did double duty—day in the school, and night with the Prince till the Prince went on an extended tour of Europe in 1938.

Retiring in 1952 or 1953, Sidq went back to his native place where he missed Hyderabad acutely. In 1961 he wrote an account of his seven-year nocturnal tenure with the Junior Prince. He passed away in 1967 at Kanpur. His only child, a daughter, migrated to Pakistan.

Sidq Jaisi was a person of medium height. He was well-built and had a wheatish complexion. His features were attractive despite pockmarks on his face. He was always well-dressed in sherwani and pajama. When he was bareheaded, one could see his well-combed hair parted in the middle. He was fond of *paan* with tobacco. He also smoked, but did not drink. Instances of lapse from teetotalism are described in the book. He was a good poet, quick-witted and with a keen sense of humour. Apart from composing poetry, he remembered by heart a large number of couplets and poems of the masters, which added to his reputation for quick-wittedness. He was, therefore, very popular with his students. When he became the warden of the school hostel, the Prince asked him how many servants he had. He replied, '13.'

'But 13 is an unlucky number,' remarked the Prince.

'I am the fourteenth,' he replied, adding, 'they are all your servants, my *Sarkar*. So am I.'

Excerpts from his book were published in various journals of India and Pakistan. He was restrained in his depiction of happenings at the Court because of a natural regard for the Prince, reinforced by the fact that the latter was still alive. Verbal tradition and the accounts of some of the incidents by the contemporaries of the Prince suggest that the book errs on the side of discretion. On the other hand, some persons question the veracity of his narration on certain points. Still, it gives an unequalled portrait of the period and the degenerate lives led by the nobility and the idle rich. It shows what superficial and false values held sway in the feudal order and how cut off the ruling class was from the lives and concerns of ordinary people.

This book is perhaps the only document of contemporary Hyderabad in the decade immediately preceding the demise of the old order. It thus shows high society in the light of the last flicker of the flame—a snapshot in a flashlight, to use an electronic metaphor. I consider it as an important historical document of the period. It is somewhat like Samuel Pepys' diary of seventeenth century England—of course with a narrower focus on life behind the velvet curtains.

The Junior Prince

The Junior Prince was a man of medium height. A dandy and a dilettante, he had a slight stammer in his speech. He and his brother had no formal schooling. They were taught by tutors at home and had acquired proficiency in Urdu, English, Persian, and Arabic.

The younger Prince—the subject of this study was, by all accounts, the more intelligent of the two, and shrewder. He was also more oriental in his outlook. He composed poetry. A slim volume of his selected poems entitled *Jazbaat-e-Shajee* was published by the Hussami Book Depot, Hyderabad, in 1983. Some of his poems are set to tune and sung in social gatherings even today. The following is a typical and popular couplet from one of his poems:

> *Woh jo mehmaan bane baithe hain*
> *Meraa imaan liye baithe hain*
>
> Sitting smugly as my guest,
> Here is the stealer of my heart.

At the time of the narrative, the two Princes received a purse of Rs 25,000 a month. There was no Income Tax in the State. But due to their improvidence, they were always in debt. The rich moneylenders would happily lend them any amount because they got IOUs from them for twice or thrice the amount of the loan. Now and then these receipts were shown to the Nizam who willy-nilly had the debts settled to avoid embarrassment. But the Princes and the Nizam himself were always exposed to the threat of blackmail because of the extravagance of the former. According to reliable sources, the Nizam had to incur an expenditure of about forty-five million rupees to wipe off the debts incurred by the two Princes. He also declared simultaneously, that thenceforth he would not be responsible for any further financial liabilities of his sons.

Muazzam Jah was forever celebrating something or the other. Apart from the traditional festivals like Eid and his birthday, which were gala affairs, there was a gathering every evening of select persons in addition to his paid and honorary courtiers. The courtiers ranged from contemporaries of his grandfather like Qudrat Nawaz Jung, whom he called 'Carew', and his teacher, 'Piya',[52] to very young persons. On occasions such as Eid, special scouts were sent to collect female singers and dancers from famous centres like Agra, Lucknow, Delhi, and Bombay (now Mumbai), and the festivities would go on for a fortnight after the festival. He also had his 'agents' stationed permanently for such procurement in Bombay. The artistes were given liberal compensation and, at the time of their departure, extravagant gifts. They were taken to the town by one of his flunkies and could buy anything they fancied on the Prince's account. One such departure of Akthari Bai Faizabadi who later became known as the celebrated Begum Akhtar is described in the book.

The Junior Prince was somewhat quick-tempered compared to his elder brother. To begin with, the Nizam was fond of him. On every Eid, he used to send a suit of clothes to his sons. While the Prince of Berar accepted them with due ceremony, the Junior Prince once returned the gift saying that the quality of cloth was not good enough for him (a similar incident is reported between the first Nizam and his rebel son Nasir Jung. It was cited as one of the contributory causes for his rebellion). The Nizam summoned his impudent son and reassured him that the suit was made of the same cloth as he used for himself.

'It may be alright for Your Exalted Highness, but not for me,' said the Prince firmly to the Nizam.

'Why?' asked the exasperated ruler.

'Because,' the Prince replied gravely but with great respect, 'Your Exalted Highness is an orphan. But my father is alive!'

The Nizam liked the repartee and, as was his wont when he appreciated something, he slapped his thigh and said, 'Indeed. Indeed. Well put.' A new suit was then given to him and the quality of future gifts improved.

Muazzam Jah had taken after his grandfather, the sixth Nizam, and remembered him fondly. His relations with his father were never very cordial and were often defiant. Nawab Shaheed Yar Jung of the Treasury Service of the State was on deputation to the Prince, first as manager of the household and later as Comptroller, the post of which he held till his retirement. Once, when the Nizam threatened to remove him from service, he mentioned this to the Prince. Muazzam Jah was enraged. He sent for the Commissioner of Police, a trusted official of the Nizam, in the presence of Shaheed Yar Jung. After his arrival, the Prince summoned one of his water carriers. The humble servant did not know why he had been called. Pointing towards him, the

Prince addressed the Commissioner of Police. 'This man is a mere water carrier. Tell your master that he cannot touch even him. Shaheed Yar Jung is a big man. Where is the question of the Nizam being able to do anything to him?' The Commissioner was stunned. The Nawab, feeling acutely embarrassed, took off his turban, and with folded hands pleaded with Muazzam Jah, for his sake, not to carry the matter so far. Once, says Khwaja Hussain Sharief 'Shouq', a poet who became his regular companion in the last two decades of his life, the Prince spent a whole night praising his grandfather and criticizing his father. Khwaja Shouq told him there could be no grandfather without a father and so he must respect him. This logic made no sense to him. A better logic was that without a grandfather there could be no father.

Colonel Khusro Yar Khan recalls a typical party in 1950. A Russian architect made the Prince's house look like a ship. Every male guest was asked to come in the guise of a pirate; every female guest dressed as a gypsy. Every table had a bottle of 'Vat 69' Scotch whisky. Khusro took a 3-tonner military vehicle 'dressed-up' as a boat. The dancing and merry-making went on until five in the morning.

The Prince was a fop. When he went to Europe, he carried 350 suits with him and earned the reputation of the best-dressed man in Europe. A typical day for the Prince would start at about 7.30 in the evening when his courtiers would start assembling. Some of them were picked up from their respective residences by cars from his fleet while the members of the nobility and higher bureaucracy came on their own. Rounds of drinks went on while the company indulged in small talk or banter by the Prince. Dinner was served between 10 p.m. and midnight. After that, the *mushaira* would start with Indian instrumental musicians and singers in attendance. It would go on till the *azan*—the morning call for prayers for the Muslims—was heard. The court was dismissed at that time. The Prince would take the last dose of sleeping tablets and retire. These tablets, a rarity in those days, were also given as a special favour to some others. His poetic preceptor, Najm Afandi, became addicted to them. When he was dismissed, therefore, his great problem was how to get his daily dose of those special sleeping pills. Later observers report that the Prince started taking the pills from midnight on so that their full effect could be felt by the time he 'rose' to sleep. The Prince would sleep till lunch, which was late in the afternoon. After lunch, he would have a nap and get up around five in the afternoon. Then he would have his shave and bath and get dressed for the 'day'.

His habit of sleeping during the forenoon was so set that when his father, the last Nizam, passed away at 1.20 in the afternoon, his ADC had to take courage in his hands and tried to wake the Prince up. Failing to get a response to his respectful requests, he whispered into his ears. 'Your Highness, I regret to submit that His Exalted Highness has expired.'

The Prince turned, and with a lazy wave of his hand, snubbed the ADC: 'Don't bring such bad news so early in the morning,' and turned on his side in deep slumber. He did not attend the funeral of his father, nor, later, of his elder brother!

Though politics did not bother him, according to the late K.M. Munshi, who served as the Agent-General of India to Hyderabad during 1947–8, the last year before the Police Action, Muazzam Jah was against his father's plans for independence for Hyderabad and even wrote to him advising merger with the Indian union.

The Prince survived the revolution as most of the leaders of the *ancien régime* did. A year after the Police Action when the Princes had ceased to hold any office, on 8 October 1949, the Nizam set up a trust with a corpus of Rs 18.2 million to provide for the Prince for the rest of his life. Muazzam Jah moved out of the Hill Fort, his official residence, went to Mumbai, bought a house on Napean Sea Road, named it 'Persipolis', and lived there till 1954. Thereafter he returned to Hyderabad. He bought a sprawling house from the Raja of Wanaparthy on Road Number 2 of Banjara Hills, and named it 'Mount Pleasant'. It now houses the Mufakkam Jah Engineering College. Later still, he shifted to 'Fern Villa' on the Red Hills which Jamaluddin, the legendary Superintendent of the Public Gardens, had built for himself and which was bought by the Nizam for the Prince and his new wife, Anwari Begum. His lifestyle continued unchanged though on a reduced scale. Anwari Begum tried in vain to impose some order on the household.

There he composed poetry and had his poems sung and admired at his soirées. The two poets Khwaja Shouq and Khumar Barabankvi belong to the last phase of his life, beginning about 1959. They did not become his courtiers. Khumar was living in Mumbai and writing lyrics for films, which made him a household name in the country. On his visits to Hyderabad, he often stayed with the Prince as his guest. Muazzam Jah did not succeed in persuading him to join him permanently. In an interview with me, Khumar recalled his lavish hospitality and his severe treatment of his servants. He used to fine them for minor lapses. Khumar often had to intercede with him on their behalf and get the fines remitted. One late afternoon Khumar was still sleeping in his room while the Prince was up and wanted some company. He asked one of his servants to go to Khumar's room and throw a Belgium glass jug on the ground. For that he would pretend to get angry and shout at him. That commotion would wake up Khumar. The conspiracy was accordingly carried out. Khumar got up due to the commotion and tried to pacify Muazzam Jah. After the burst of mock-anger, the Prince became morose. He started strolling on the terrace of 'Mount Pleasant'. From that height, he could see the whole city spread at his feet. The evening lights made it look like an inverted sky with stars strewn all over. Khumar asked the Prince the reason for his low spirits. Muazzam Jah pointed at the lighted city and said: 'How times have changed! There was a time when all this belonged to us. And now ...!' Khumar offered him solace. 'Nothing stays as it was, Sarkar', he said, 'except the name and glory of Allah.'

Muazzam Jah's improvidence continued despite Anwari Begum's restraint. Once in Mumbai, when the Prince was staying at Hotel President, Khumar went to see him. He saw the Prince literally held captive by two young Marwaris. They were abusively demanding the discharge of their debt. The Prince told Khumar to come the next evening, and, to Khumar's shock, added, 'Bring your own paans.'

Khumar sent a message to Anwari Begum in Hyderabad. She reached Mumbai and had her husband 'released' from his debtors. The Prince along with his retinue of about twenty then moved to Raj Bhavan, which was then occupied by Nawab Ali Yawar Jung who in the 1930s had been once Comptroller of the Prince's household.

Muazzam Jah's health began to fail in the early 1980s. First, he started leaning on a stick for walking. Later, it was a pitiable sight to see the flamboyant Prince of olden days leaning on human shoulders to walk up to meet his visitors. On 15 September 1987, too weak to write himself, he dictated five 'salaams' (devotional poems dedicated to Imam Husain) to his son, Shahamat Jah. Later, he had them read to him. Ali Pasha, his lifelong friend and the husband of his stepsister, was to go to Calcutta to attend a board meeting of a company. Muazzam Jah called him and asked him whether he could stay back. Ali Pasha readily cancelled his journey. Khwaja 'Shouq' was also asked by the family to stay on for the night. He could not; his own family would get worried if he did not return home at night. He noted, however, that Muazzam Jah's speech had become indistinct. At about

10.45 p.m. he became restless and then lapsed into a coma. Mir Shujat Ali Khan, Wala Shan Prince Muazzam Jah Bahadur then breathed his last. In his own words:

> Thus was completed the journey of love.
> Often the destinations came to greet me.

Next day, as his cortège moved out, an observer counted thirteen mourners in all. The man who had entertained thousands in his life and never had a meal with less than a score went to his grave practically alone. Ali Pasha, in a touching gesture gave away the grave, which he had got reserved for himself, in the Daira-e-Mir Momin Graveyard, to his old friend for his eternal rest. With his death was closed, forever, the last of the feudal, glittering, nocturnal courts of India.

In this book, we see a picture of the age. The feudal system and its grandees are portrayed here. The atmosphere in the 'courts', the sycophancies, intrigues, and the empty chatter of courtiers is described artlessly. Also described in varying degrees of detail are some of the leading lights of that period. Amongst the leading poets of the twentieth century, we meet Josh Maleehabadi,[53] the 'poet of revolution', and Fani, 'the poet of gloom'.[54] We see Najm Afandi, the poetic tutor of the Prince, falling from grace in a whimsical and arbitrary manner. We meet the celebrated singer Begum Akhtar in her early days when she was merely Akhtari Bai Faizabadi, performing and collecting a booty. We hear the story of the appointment of Dagh as the poetic preceptor of the sixth Nizam on a mere whim of the ruler after a frustrating wait of ten long years. We meet the eccentric Police Minister, Shahab Jung, almost in flesh and blood. We also witness his tragic end. We are given glimpses of Maharaja Kishen Pershad and his minister, Nawab Mehdi Yar Jung. We meet a host of characters. Some are etched in detail. Others are thumbnail sketches. Some evoke admiration, some scorn, others pity—but all of them interest. While most characters are real, some, like Ummak Jung and Dhimmak Jung (the Indian equivalent of Tom, Dick, and Harry) are deliberately presented as prototypes so as not to offend some of the people who were still alive. But informed opinion holds that one of these two characters was based on Nawab Hosh Yar Jung who was a glib talker and a close confidant of the Nizam. He himself later wrote a somewhat unflattering book in Urdu about his master and his times called *Mushahidaat* (Observations). Some of his observations in the first edition were later deleted to avoid the Nizam embarrassment. We learn about the superstition of the Asaf Jahi Dynasty because of which a waiter in the Taj Hotel of Mumbai acquires a fortune overnight. We see how much obsequiousness and non-stop flattery were the chief ingredients of the survival kit in the court. We are also shown the great contrast between the ornate and extravagant lifestyle of the Prince, and the austere court of his father, the last Nizam, who was reputedly the world's richest man of his times.

This book constitutes, as it were, a case study of the princely order of India. It shows high life in the largest Princely State of India close to its twilight. It is the picture largely of life within the four walls of a false Camelot, an artificial cocoon. Outside these walls, a storm was raging, a new order was struggling to be born, and a new dawn was about to arrive. These people, like the Sun King and Marie Antoinette of France, were unaware of the approaching revolution. The book is a procession of silhouettes thrown up by the last flicker of a flame. The surprise is that it was happening in the twentieth century—in our own lifetime!

Moulvi Abdul Haq,[55] 'Father of Urdu', in a letter to the author, commended the book. He said, 'Your book is a rare thing. The attractive style, in which you have given an account of the court of the Prince and his nobles, will confer upon it a historical status. It was the last court. Now there will be neither such princes, nor such courts—nor even writers like you. I am sure that this book will prove very popular and acquire a special status in Urdu literature.'[56]

As pointed out by Abdul Majid Daryabadi in his foreword to the book, the whole narrative is a fairy tale described by an imp who happened to get a peep into it, and who was a good raconteur. Prometheus-like, he has stolen a picture of a false heaven, and distributed it to the world.

Some people allege that the author has distorted facts, and the account given by him is negative and tends to hold the court and the Prince to ridicule and contempt. The compiler of Sidq Jaisi's biography, Mohammad Noor-ud-Din Khan, has rebutted this point. He says that when the book was published, many of the courtiers and friends of the Prince were alive.

They included poets and writers. They could have pointed out factual inaccuracies through some article or even written books giving their own version. No one did that. Further, he says that though Sidq Jaisi belonged to the north, he followed the traditions of the Deccan and kept the dignity of the Prince in view. He did not exceed the limits of etiquette and refrained from ridicule. 'If *Darbaar-e-Dürbaar* had not been published, we the people of Hyderabad would have remained ignorant of the conditions prevalent in the court of Prince Muazzam Jah just as we are ignorant of the darbars and nobles of the Deccan.'[57]

This introduction is intended to provide a historical context to an interesting story, which bears out the old saying that sometimes truth is stranger than fiction.

NARENDRA LUTHER

Notes

[1] For a detailed description, see the two volumes of J. Irvine, *The Later Mughals*, (New Delhi, New Taj Publishers and Distributors, 1989).

[2] This has been translated and edited by E.S. Harcourt and Fakhir Hussain and published as a part of *The Lucknow Omnibus* by Abdul Halim Sharar, Rosie Llewellyn-Jones and Veena Talwar Oldenburg (New Delhi, Oxford University Press, 2001).

[3] Arabic muttah, enjoyment; marriages contracted for a limited period, usually in exchange for some monetary consideration on the part of the woman. It was frequently practised in the past among wealthy Shias. This note is given in the original text.

[4] Music as well as other forms of intoxication are important prohibitions of Islam. This note is given in the original text.

[5] *The Lucknow Omnibus*, p. 71.

[6] There are many biographical accounts of the First Asaf Jah. The best and the most detailed is *The First Nizam: Life and Times of Nizam-ul-Mulk Asaf Jah I* by Yusuf Hussain (Delhi, Asia Publishing House, 1963).

[7] P. Setu Madhava Rao, *Eighteenth Century Deccan* (Bombay, Popular Prakshan, 1963), p. 106.

[8] Ibid., p. 106.

[9] Ibid., p. 64.

[10] Eenugula Veeraswamy, 1831, trans. and ed. by P. Sitapati and V. Puryshottam. 1973, p. 25.

[11] Ibid., p. 120.

[12] Quoted by the author in his *Memoirs of a City* (Hyderabad, Orient Longman, 1995), p. 171.

[13] Mushtaq Hussain, *Gulgasht-e-Deccan*, quoted in *Mamlakat-e-Asafiya* (Karachi, Idara-e-Muhibban-e-Deccan, 1978, vol. 11), p. 201.

[14] Nawab Jiwan Yar Jung Bahadur, *My Life—Being the Autobiography of Nawab Server-ul-Mulk Bahadur*, trans. from the Urdu (London, Arthur H. Stockwell, undated), p. 150.

[15] See author's article, 'The Nizam as Poet and Publisher' in *The Hindu*, 27 September 1998.

[16] A mushaira is an elaborate ritual for the recitation of the *ghazal* (poetry of love) genre of Urdu poetry. Traditionally, the poets dressed in formal buttoned-up long coats called *sherwani* and tight trousers called *churidar pajama*, sat in a semi-circle on a white sheet covering a wooden platform raised about two feet above the ground. They had bolsters for back support. The poets numbered usually about a dozen and chewed *paans* (betel leaves filled with special ingredients). The function started usually about 9 p.m. and went on till the wee hours of the morning. The poets were called in order of juniority—the masters coming at the end. The head poet who sat in the middle of the semi-circle invited the poets and said a few words of praise about them. A lighted lamp called *shama* was placed before the poet who recited his poem. Some poets 'sang' their poems. This is called *tarannum*. The mushaira was either *tarhi* in which poems were required to be set to a given scheme of rhyme and metre, or *ghair-tarhi*, that is free from rhyme and metre. The latter form gave better scope for the poet to display his virtuosity. The audience was encouraged to shout exclamations of praise and good couplets earned repeated encores. Lately, mushairas have become informal and in many cases, a professional master of ceremonies is hired to conduct the proceedings. They are held in the open and thousands of people pay to attend them, if there are good poets to listen to. For a detailed exposition of the subject, see Isaac Sequeira's article, 'The Mystique of the Mushaira' published in *The Journal of Popular Culture* (Bowling Green, USA, 1981, vol. 15, no. 1).

[17] This view finds acknowledgement in Mohammad Sadiq, *A History of Urdu Literature* (New Delhi, Oxford University Press, 1984), p. 51; Dr Zore, *Dakni Adab ki Tarikh* (Hyderabad, Idara-e-Adabiyat-e-Urdu, 1959).

[18] Masud Husain Khan, *Dakhi-Urdu* in *Medieval History of India*, ed. H.K. Sherwani (Hyderabad, 1974).

[19] Jan Pieper, *Hyderabad: A Quranic Paradise in Architectural Metaphors in Environmental Design*, ed. A. Peruccioli (Genzano de Roma: Environmental Design, The Journal of the Islamic Environmental Design Research Centre, January 1983), pp. 46–51.

[20] Abbé Carre, *The Travels of Abbé Carré in India in the New East 1672–74* (1674, 2 vols, reprinted, New Delhi, Asian Educational Services, 1990), p. 329.

[21] William Irvine, *A Pepys of Mogul India—1653–1708—Being an Abridged edition of the 'Storia Do Mogor of Niccolao Manucci'* (1913, reprint, New Delhi, Low Price Publication, 1996), pp. 193–5.

[22] S.P. Shorey, *Architecture of Andhra Pradesh* (A.P. Government official website).

[23] Raza Ali Khan, *Hyderabad—A City in History*, published by the author, 1986, pp. 56–7.

[24] Val. C. Prinsep, *Imperial India—An Artist's Journals* (London, Chapman and Hall, undated), p. 317.

[25] Based on the note by Ms Lakshmi Devi Raj, an expert in the dress designs of Hyderabad.

[26] *Mamlakat-e-Asafiya* (Karachi, Idara-e-Muhibban-e-Deccan, vol. 11), pp. 372–86.

[27] Mehdi Nawaz Jung, *Maharaja Kishen Pershad* (Hyderabad, 1950), p. 91.

[28] Mohiuddin Qadri Zore, quoted by Mohd. Azeez-ud-Din Mohiuddin Mohabbat in *Mamlakat-e-Asafiya* (Karachi, Idara-e-Muhibban-e-Deccan, 1989, vol. II), p. 365.

[29] Nawab Jivan Yar Jung Bahadur, p. 92.

[30] For an account of the way the Residency was built, and its grandeur, see H.G. Briggs, *The Nizam: His History and Relations with the British Government* (2 vols, London, Bernard Quaritch and John William Kaye, 1861). Also *Life and Correspondence of Major General John Malcolm* (London, Smith Elder & Co., 1856), pp. 100–1.

[31] Karen Isaken Leonard, 'British Impact on Hyderabad' essay in the *Studies in the Foreign Relations of India (From the earliest times to 1947)*, Prof. H.K. Sherwani Felicitation Volume, ed. P.M. Joshi (1975), p. 448.

[32] Ibid., p. 451.

[33] For a description of the party, see the author's *Memoirs of a City* (Hyderabad, Orient Longman, 1995), pp. 217–20.

[34] See for example his poem in Syeda Jaffer, *Kulliyat-e-Mohammad Quli Qutb Shah* (New Delhi, Taraqqui-e-Urdu Board, 1985), p. 754.

[35] Karen Isaken Leonard, *Social History of an Indian Caste: The Kayasths of Hyderabad* (Califonia, reprinted, Hyderabad, Orient Longman,1994), p. 123. There

is a difference of dates between Leonard and Manak Rao Vithal Rao's *Bostan-e-Asafiya* (Hyderabad, Chistia Press, 1925), and Rai Satguru Pershad, *Farkhunda Buniyad Hyderabad* (Intekhab Press, undated), (Both in Urdu).

[36] Manak Rao Vithal Rao, 1909–32. *Bostan-e-Asafiya* in 8 vols, vol. II, pp. 750–52 quoted by Dr Vandana Kaushik in 'Religious and Cultural Synthesis in the Nineteenth Century Hyderabad', paper presented at the Indian History Art and Culture Society (Kanyakumari, November, 1990).

[37] Harriet Ronken Lynton, and Mohini Rajan, *The Days of the Beloved* (Los Angeles, University of California Press, 1974), p. 16.

[38] Leonard, *Social History of an Indian Caste: The Kayasths of Hyderabad*, pp. 81–2.

[39] The full text of his speech, kindly made available to the author by his son, the late Rasheed-ud-Din Khan, is with the author. A report of the speech appeared in *The Hindu* of 13 August 1936.

[40] Vithal Rao, *Bostan-e-Asafiya*, vol. II, pp. 756–7.

[41] D.F. Karaka, *History of the Parsis* (London, Macmillan & Co., 1884, vol. II), p. 184.

[42] Eckehard Kulke, *The Parsis in India: A Minority as Agent of Social Change* (New Delhi, Vikas, 1978), p. 81.

[43] D.N. Varma, 'Composite Nature of Hyderabadi Culture', paper read at the Inter-Cultural Cooperation (India, Hyderabad Chapter, 20–21 January, 1990), pp. 8–9.

[44] This incident was narrated by his son, Pandit Jasraj, at a private sitting in Hyderabad on 6 September 1998.

[45] Varma, p. 9.

[46] Ibid., p. 14.

[47] Letter of Sarojini Naidu in Jawaharlal Nehru, *A Bunch of Old Letters* (Oxford, Oxford University Press, 1958), p. 44.

[48] Philip Mason, *A Shaft of Sunlight—Memoirs of a Varied Life* (New Delhi, Vikas, 1978), p. 200.

[49] As narrated to the author by Janaki Pershad's son, Mohan Prasad. Quoted in the author's *Hyderabad: Memoirs of a City* (Hyderabad, Orient Longman, 1995), pp. 344–5.

[50] Nawab Mirza Dagh, the celebrated Urdu poet (1831–1905). Through his mother's second marriage, he became a grandson of the last Mughal emperor, Bahadur Shah Zafar (accession 1837, deposed 1857). Immediately after the Mutiny, he moved to Rampur where he was appointed companion to the heir apparent, Nawab Kalab Ali Khan. When, on his death in 1886, the court poet was dismissed by the Regency, Dagh came to Hyderabad. There he became the poetic preceptor to the sixth Nizam. The story of his appointment is described later.

[51] Hafiz Jaleel Hasan, Jaleel Manakpuri (1862–1946) came from Rampur in 1900. He had to wait for nine years before he was appointed as the poetic preceptor to Nizam VI in 1909 to succeed Dagh who had died in 1905. On the death of the sixth Nizam in 1911, he continued with his son, the last Nizam. He had thus the distinction of serving as the poetic preceptor of two Nizams. He was given the title of Nawab Fasahat Jung. He died in 1946. The full story of his appointment is described in my book *Memoirs of a City* (Hyderabad, Orient Longman, 1995).

[52] Pet name used by the Prince for Nawab Nasir-ud-Dowla.

[53] Shabbir Hasan Khan 'Josh Maleehabadi' was born in Uttar Pradesh (UP) in 1898, in a well-to-do family. He came from a line of poets. He had socialist leanings and was fiercely anti-British. According to his autobiography, he had a dream in which the Prophet Mohammad told him that he would live under the patronage of the Nizam for ten years. In 1924, armed with letters of recommendation from the famous poet, Dr Mohammad Iqbal and Akbar Allahabadi, he landed in Hyderabad. Recommended to Sir Akbar Hydari, he insulted him when the former asked him whether he could add to the numerous panegyrics about him. However, he was appointed to the Bureau of Translation of Osmania University where he served for ten years. Once, on the Nizam's birthday, he wrote a poem in which he said that rather than the Nizam, he, that is Josh, should be eulogized. He followed up that poem with one in which he attacked the feudal system. It was recited in a gathering which was attended by the leading nobles of Hyderabad. Because of these acts of insolence, he was sacked and asked to leave the state within fifteen days. According to Josh, he was offered a pardon if he apologized. However, according to the records in the State Archives of Andhra Pradesh (AP), he sought pardon but the Nizam refused to grant it.

It was a rule in Hyderabad that a person expelled from the State was given a pension of Rs 100 a month. Josh also was given that. But he said that he did not have money for undertaking the journey out of Hyderabad. So he was given a special grant of Rs 1000 for that purpose.

In 1943 and again in 1947, Josh petitioned to the Nizam to visit Hyderabad. The Nizam rejected both. He migrated to Pakistan, returned to India, and again went back. He did not get the recognition which he expected from the Government of Pakistan. He visited Hyderabad in 1962 when I, unaware of the background, organized an official reception for him. He died in Pakistan in 1982, a frustrated and embittered man.

There are two conflicting accounts of his exit from Hyderabad. His version is given in his autobiography, *Yadon Ki Barat* (first published in Pakistan, 1970; Indian edition, Lucknow, Aino-e-Adab, 1973).

The other version, based on official records in the State Archives, is given by Dr Syed Dawood Ashraf in his book *Auaraq-e-Muarrikh* (Hyderabad, Shagoofa Publications, 1998), pp. 29–48.

[54] Showkat Ali Khan, Fani Badayuni (1879–1941), an outstanding poet of morbidity whose poetry is a perpetual reminder of death. He believed that Fate was responsible for all his—and others'—miseries. His strong point is style—concentrated, firm, at once scholarly and simple.

[55] Moulvi Abdul Haq, also known as the grand old man of Urdu, was a professor in Osmania University. He was a great scholar and compiled a dictionary of Urdu. There is an interesting incident about his encounter with the Nizam. Some sycophant courtiers of the Nizam suggested that his poetic compositions should be prescribed as part of the syllabus for the graduate course in Urdu. The Nizam issued orders accordingly. Moulvi Abdul Haq was the professor of Urdu at Osmania University. He became alarmed at the likely ridicule that would be heaped upon him in the academic world by such an act. He approached the Nizam and in a very ingenious way, convinced him that the level of his compositions was so high that even teachers were not able to comprehend them. How then would they be able to explicate them to the students? Puffed by such praise, the Nizam agreed to have the orders postponed. For a full account of the incident, see my book, *Memoirs of a City*.

[56] Mohammad Noor-ud-Din Khan, *Sidq Jaisi* (Hyderabad, Adabistan-e-Deccan, 1994), p. 141.

[57] Ibid., p. 142.

Prologue

TIMES CHANGE. The world does not always abide by us. I had read about the decline of the Qutb Shahi dynasty in history books; the rise and fall of the Asaf Jahi dynasty I saw with my own eyes. Hyderabad was not a place one would have left easily. But sometimes one is helpless. At last, I had to depart from that city, every brick and stone of which I loved. In the last week of November 1953, I departed from the bride of cities in which I had lived a life of peace and contentment for twenty-six years. My heart was heavy and my eyes were moist.

If Nawab Kazim Jung[1] had kept his word, I would probably never have left Hyderabad. But I was fated to write this book. Because of that, destiny sent me once again in my old age to Jais—a place once renowned for scholarship but now ruled by witlessness and illiteracy.

To cope with the lack of society, and my loneliness at home, I thought of occupying myself by writing about the richness of the capital of the Hyderabad State, the old language of the Deccan, its customs and traditions, and the rise and fall of the Asafiya[2] dynasty. The book is a mirror in which the ruler and his ministers, the nobles and the notables are reflected in their true colours. Nobody is unduly praised, but neither is anyone spared. I had the proud distinction to be the first of the poets of the north to go to the Deccan at the beginning of the twentieth century. I mean those of us who were destined one day to have the privilege of the companionship and honorary courtiership of the Junior Prince, Muazzam Jah.

One fine morning in the spring of 1923, a slow train of the Nizam's Railways took me via Manmad to the Kachiguda station of Hyderabad. I had informed Fasahat Jung Jaleel, the poetic instructor of the Nizam VII about my arrival earlier. His sister's son Nisar (who was probably a *peshkar* in Medak district) was there to receive me. My baggage was put in the buggy by the syce and I was driven home. Jaleel's house was an ornate building in the old style in the heart of the city. It had both electricity and running water—rare amenities at the time. The outer portion of the house had a large hall and two rooms. The hall served as a drawing room and, at prayer times, as a mosque. In front of the hall was a small verandah in which after the Morning Prayer the royal tutor would sit in an easy chair and count the rosary. One of the side rooms was allotted to me.

I fell in love with the new city at first sight, though the city of those days was vastly different from what it is today. At that time, there were neither wide beautiful roads nor any streetlights. The roads were nevertheless so full of carts and bicycles that I used to call it the city of vehicles. The natives of the city were very sincere, hospitable, and sociable. The language spoken there at that time was that which the readers will come across my friend, the Colonel, speaking in this book.[3]

I remained a pupil of Jaleel for about eight months. In another portion of the house in which Jaleel was staying was the residence of Nawab Akhtar Yar Jung (Akhtar Meenai), son of the celebrated poet Ameer Meenai. He was Secretary of the Department of Ecclesiastic Affairs. After toiling eight months, I was able to obtain a *mulki* certificate. Hardly had I obtained this passport for a job when plague broke out in the city. I had to therefore willy-nilly return empty-handed to my native place.

Two or three years after my return, my kind friend Josh Maleehabadi, the poet, landed in Hyderabad. God alone knows where he stayed or whom he met because I was then in Bhopal. I came to know only this that Nawab Imadul Mulk[4] recommended him and Qader Nawaz Jung[5] presented him to the Nizam. There is a good joke about his admittance to the presence but I will not write about it here because Josh himself will narrate it better in his autobiography.[6]

I returned to the Deccan towards the close of 1927. In 1928, I was appointed to the *Dar-ul-uloom* on the special orders of Maharaja Sir Kishen Pershad.[7]

Some years after my appointment, Fani came to Hyderabad through the efforts of Josh Maleehabadi and stayed for many months at the Aziz Company as the guest of the government. After that, he was appointed headmaster of the Darul Shifa High School, on the orders of the Maharaja.

After this appointment, Mahirul Qadri, probably through the good offices of Abdul Qadeer Badayuni, came to Hyderabad in the prime of his youth and was appointed to the High Court on the orders of the Maharaja.

The distinction of joining the court of the Junior Prince, Muazzam Jah Bahadur, came first to Josh. He in turn took Fani there. After Fani came Mahir. I do not know how he obtained that honour. After that, Najm[8] came through Nawab Shaheed Yar Jung. Najm was the poetry tutor of the Junior Prince and was thus his paid employee. I was the last to enter the court. It was Fani who dragged me to it and details of that are described in the book.

Of all the courtiers of the Junior Prince, only these five poets are worth mentioning. They came with honour and left in good grace. There were many others too but I omit to mention them because they shone in that distinguished court for a short while like fireflies and then went into oblivion.

The names of the courtiers mentioned in the book are real. Only two, Ummak Jung and Dhimmak Jung, are fictional characters. They are the prototypes of those nobles who made their appearance in the court off and on. They wasted their nights in mushairas. They were neither poets, nor did they comprehend poetry. Everybody knew that they recited others' compositions and praised poems to the skies without understanding them. They did all this just to survive in the court. I do not say anything about anyone except repeat *sotto voce* the famous remark of the editor of the *Avadh Punch*[9] that 'whomsoever this paper cap fits is a fool'.

SIDQ JAISI (MIRZA TASSADUQ HUSSAIN)
Kothi Shahzad Sahib
Rai Bareli (UP)

Notes

[1] Popularly known as Ali Pasha. He was the favourite son-in-law of the seventh Nizam. He passed away on 25 May 1996. The nature of the 'word' referred to here could not be ascertained. Probably it was in connection with an extension of services or for a job.

[2] The Asaf Jahi dynasty.

[3] Dakhni (or Deccani), the original form of Urdu in the south. About its development, see p. xxx. Now it is reduced to a dialect. In some aspects of its grammar and syntax, it has considerable resemblance to Punjabi. It has a large vocabulary drawn from Punjabi. It imbibed some vocabulary from the southern languages too, but not to the same extent as from Punjabi. To the modern non-Dakhni ear, used to the Urdu of the north, it sounds a little odd and amusing.

[4] Syed Hussain Bilgrami (1842–1926) belonged to UP. Sir Salar Jung I brought him to Hyderabad as his secretary. Later, he became a tutor and secretary to the sixth Nizam. Thereafter he became the Director of Education of the State. In that capacity, he established a number of schools and colleges including the Nizam College, as also the Asafiya Library, now called the State Central Library. When the Advisory Council to the Secretary of State for India was established, he was selected to serve on that. He was knighted by the British and given the title of *Imad-ul-Mulk* (Pillar of the State) by the Nizam. He was the pater familias of the powerful Bilgrami clan of Hyderabad whose members occupied key positions in government for three generations.

[5] His original name was Abdul Qader. He was Collector of Nalgonda district, and later Commissioner of Gulbarga division. After retirement, he was appointed to the private estate of the Nizam called '*Sarf-e-Khas*'. Informed opinion is that he was not the sort of person to have any influence over the Nizam. Most probably, the author is confusing him with Nawab Qudrat Nawaz Jung who was the brother of the wife of the seventh Nizam and who figures later in this book.

[6] The autobiography of Josh Maleehabadi called *Yadon Ki Barat* was published in Urdu in 1970. It was banned in Pakistan. It is available in the paperback edition of Hind Pocket Books, Shahdara, Delhi. Also, see note 53 in the Introduction.

[7] Maharaja Sir Kishen Pershad was Prime Minister of Hyderabad 1900–12 and President of the Executive Council 1925–36. He was himself a poet and a patron of arts and letters.

[8] Mirza Tajammul Hussain Najm Afandi (1893–1975).

[9] A famous humorous journal published from Lucknow from 1877 to 1912. It was edited by Murtuza Sajjad Hussain who died in 1912.

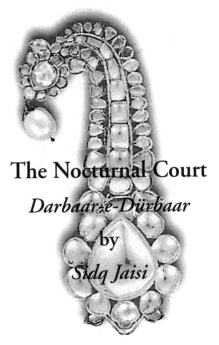

The Nocturnal Court
Darbaar-e-Durbaar

by

Sidq Jaisi

Fani in Hyderabad Deccan

JOSH ALWAYS BEGAN his conversation with something startling. One day he suddenly said: 'Fani is very upset these days. He has no work in Agra [he meant legal practice]. He has written many letters to me about his straitened circumstances. I am thinking of speaking to the Maharaj [Kishen Pershad] and getting him here.' I endorsed the idea and there the matter ended. Weeks passed into months and the topic was never raised again. Six or seven months later, one evening I visited Josh at his house. In front of him was a delicately cut piece of board on which fine lines were drawn. He was very happy to see me and said, 'You have come at the right time. This is a planchette. You can call up any spirit through this and talk to it.'

I looked at the object carefully. It had two small wheels at the broad end and a pencil stuck in the narrow front. Josh handed the pencil to a young boy, placed a sheet of plain paper in front of him and addressed the contraption: 'I want to talk to the spirit of Hafiz Shirazi [the famed Persian poet].' After he had repeated this sentence thrice, the pencil started writing. Josh's face brightened. He told me in a hushed tone that the spirit had responded. He greeted it and then asked:

'How are you doing?'

'I am quite well,' the pencil wrote.

'You have no trouble?'

'None.'

After many such questions, Josh asked: 'My friend Fani is in dire straits. Should I call him to Hyderabad?' Came the reply: 'Yes, call him. He will get a job here. But he will have to wait.'

I noted that the reply excited Josh and the hesitation that he had in calling Fani seemed to disappear. This was the second occasion when he remembered Fani. After that Khaqani, Anwari, Qaane, Urfi, Saadi, Khusro, Firduasi (all famous Persian poets and men of letters) and the spirits of various other luminaries were summoned and Josh appeared reassured with their replies.

Sometimes it happened that Josh would summon the spirit of Omar Khayyam[1] and the pencil would write 'Satan'. Annoyed, Josh would ask why Satan had taken the trouble to come. The reply would be: 'No trouble at all. I am always with you.' This would cause great amusement and all the friends present would break into guffaws. Josh would join them.

This diversion continued for months while Fani suffered in Agra. Finally, Josh made the submission to Maharaja Bahadur and obtained his approval for asking Fani to Hyderabad.

Fani arrived and under orders of the Maharaja he was put up at Aziz Company. The Maharaja enjoyed his poetry immensely and kept praising it for a long time.

Fani was staying in the upstairs portion of Aziz Company. He could order his meals and tea twice daily any time on the house. But the thought of his family living indigently in Agra worried him. There was a more serious problem. Sons of the idle rich who had nothing to do except gallivant, play bridge, or gossip found a new avocation. They started dropping in to see Fani at all times of the day. Fani felt specially pestered by two young nawabs. He was expected to entertain them according to their status and he had not the means to do so. Josh knows better than me how this problem was tackled. But within two weeks, a small but airy house of the City Improvement Board was arranged for Fani at a rent of Rs 10 per month. Fani then shifted to the Mallapelly locality of the city.

Maharaja Kishen Pershad granted an allowance of Rs 200 per month for Fani from his own pocket. This enabled Fani to send for his family, which consisted of his wife and two sons, Feroz Ali Khan and Wajahat Ali Khan. Both the boys were grown up but their only occupation was to read novels, play carom, or loaf around. They did not do anything. Of the two, Wajahat Ali Khan had read a couple of books on medicine; Feroz Khan did not acquire any learning or skill.

Now Fani started attending the Maharaja's court every day. Perhaps at the instance of Josh, the Maharaja sponsored him for the post of *munsif* (judicial magistrate). Fani was a law graduate and so the proposal was appropriate. If he had accepted it, he would certainly have retired as a judge. But fate had willed that he live his life without adequate food or medicine.

Fani did not accept the offer of that post because that would have meant being posted out of Hyderabad and he would miss the society of the city. He was a lover of company and it is this same society which exhibited criminal neglect towards him. Fani was mistaken in his assessment of society. Society requires wealth and ease of circumstances and he did not have them.

The Maharaja Bahadur was informed of Fani's unwillingness to leave the city. In the circumstances, he could only be appointed as headmaster at the Darulshifa High School. He accepted the post gladly.

There is a saying in Hyderabad that when misfortune befalls a horse he is yoked to a cart: when it befalls a man, he is appointed in the education department. That was the beginning. Fani had to produce a mulki certificate (of domicile in Hyderabad). Without that, the audit department would not release his salary. Then there was the question of age. The age limit for joining government service was 30 years. Fani was already 50 years old. An application for exemption from both these conditions was submitted to the Nizam. He objected that if outsiders were appointed to such ordinary jobs, where would the educated natives go?

When this objection became public knowledge, the newspapers in the city blew it up. For months, a spate of articles were published against 'outsiders'. In due course, the storm blew over and on the special recommendation of the Maharaja, both exemptions were granted.

A period of contentment followed for Fani. He was getting a salary of Rs 250 for the post and a stipend of Rs 200 from the Maharaja. But he disturbed things by borrowing money from the School Society for the purchase of a car. That resulted in a deduction of Rs 100 every month from his salary. Another Rs 100 went in the driver's salary and fuel for the car. So the net amount he got from his salary was a mere Rs 50 or so.

So Fani had to subsist on the stipend from the Maharaja. He could have managed comfortably. But a life of peace and quiet was not for him. Josh pushed him to the court of the Junior Prince thinking he was doing Fani a favour. But this favour proved fatal for Fani in the end. The Prince's court was held at night. Attendance at the court was ostensibly an honour but at the price of keeping awake the whole night. Fani had to suffer this ordeal for fifteen years continuously.

For a man above 50 years, keeping awake the whole night would take its toll. Generally Fani would be relieved from the court at about 4.00 in the morning. He would then go to sleep, and with great difficulty could get up only at 10.00 a.m. Getting ready hurriedly, he would reach school at 11.00 a.m. His work at the school naturally began to suffer. Reports started reaching the Inspector of Schools that Fani reached school not before 11.00 a.m. and that once there, he lounged in the office in an easy chair.

Fani thought everyone as gentlemanlike as himself. He would narrate with great relish the merriments of the court to those whom he considered his well-wishers. He did not realize that there were jealous people amongst apparent friends. Some of those people would carry tales to the Inspector of Schools in the evening.

These complaints had their effect. However, the Inspector had to put up with Fani because the latter had the backing of the Prime Minister.

But here too, attendance at the Prince's court was at the cost of attendance at the court of the Maharaja. Unfortunately Fani considered the courtiership of the Prince more important though it amounted to nothing more than insomnolence and idle praise.

Five years passed in this hard labour and Fani reached age 55, which was the age of superannuation. The Department retired him. But the Maharaja was still the Prime Minister. He gave him an extension of five years.

Two years later, the Maharaja ceased to be the Prime Minister and retreated into his mansion. For Fani the whole world changed with this. Now the officers of the Education Department started cold-shouldering him. The Inspector of Schools who had earlier been forced to be polite became brusque with him. Within a month, Fani was transferred to a *tahsil* of Nanded district. There, apart from the head of the tahsil and the munsif, no educated person was to be met with. On the strong advice of friends, Fani reported there but he returned within a week unable to adjust to the lack of society. He applied for sick leave, which entitled one to half salary but took months to be sanctioned. So Fani had to fall back upon the stipend of Rs 200 which he was still getting from the Maharaja.

Fani became resigned to his fate. Since there was nothing else to do, his sole occupation was the nocturnal court of the Prince. This pattern of life against nature took its toll. He fell prey to numerous diseases and needed medication. Free medication was available only at government hospitals and Fani's status would not allow him to accept that charity. Through the day, Fani would try in vain to pump some energy into his system by cup after cup of tea. At night, he would get some pep from the sumptuous dinner with the Prince. But that fuel would be expended by the time he left the court early in the morning.

These sittings, which were called mushairas, were where he wasted his time. I shall describe these gatherings separately later.

Fani's income had fallen steeply but there was no reduction in his expenses. The driver's salary and expenditure on petrol were fixed expenditures. In order to meet these expenses Fani started borrowing from moneylenders.

In the evening Fani would go for a spin in his car trying to forget his miseries in the fresh air of the Public Garden. He believed that one day the Prince would pay off all his debts and thus relieve him of his worries. Some of his friends also entertained similar hopes.

Every fourth or fifth month Fani would get his accumulated arrears of half pay but they could not help discharge the debt. They were barely enough for groceries, vegetables, and other daily necessities. Meanwhile the loan amount kept on increasing. When Fani became convinced that he was going to sink, he said to himself; 'Why go down alone; why not have a companion in adversity? That would alleviate the feeling of loneliness.' For that purpose, he picked on me.

It happened this way. One night Fani recited a ghazal, which the Prince liked very much. Fani made his customary numerous bows to acknowledge the praise and said that in that style of ghazal, his friend Sidq Jaisi had written a masterpiece. Then he recited my couplet:

Us ke lutf-e-aam ko ghairat nahin karti kabool
Aur main kambakhat lutf-e-khaas ke kaabil nahin

Self-respect will not accept her favours commonplace,
But I, the unfortunate don't deserve her special grace.

The couplet was good. The Prince was exhilarated by it. He asked his poetry instructor, Najm Afandi, to fetch me the next evening.

The next day Najm suddenly appeared at my house. I thought it was a courtesy call. After the exchange of civilities, he came to the purpose of his visit and asked me to get ready immediately. I will describe my induction into the court in due course.

Thus Fani pulled me into the eddy in which he himself had been struggling for life for about ten years. From then on, in addition to meeting him during the daytime, I began to spend my nights also with him at the court.

So I shared his vigil for seven years continuously and there is no one who watched him more closely than I. None can therefore describe as truly his tragic end as I can.

Whatever happened to that great poet in that abode of wealth called Hyderabad I shall narrate accurately.

The First Night at the Court

A WHOLE SEPARATE BOOK would be needed to describe the beauty and opulence of the palace of the Prince, called the 'Hill Fort'. My entire life has been spent with the rich and the noble. But as I stepped out of the car in the compound of the Hill Fort Palace, which was surrounded by a high green hedge, I was simply overawed by its grandeur. I was so nervous that I wanted simply to turn back and not face the Prince. But with Najm there, it was not possible.

On the vast ground in which the car pulled up, the spread of red gravel in the light of the lamps seemed like a colourful carpet of flowers. Najm asked me to follow him. I submitted nervously. We climbed three or four steps and entered a gallery, which had wall-to-wall matting. A tall Negro called 'Siddi' in local parlance stood immobile with a gun in hand. At that time, when my heart was beating fast, I took him to be a statue. After walking a few steps, Najm turned to the right and entered a large hall in which a number of officers and nobles in glittering dress, wearing bagloos and dastar were sitting on costly chairs and sofas. On seeing us, they got up and came up to shake our hands. I found that except for three or four, most of them were my acquaintances. Fani was first to walk up to me, beaming at the success of his plan and shook me by the hand. His presence gave me some confidence and I sat down by his side. He congratulated me on my good fortune. Others followed him with the same message. In those days, it was really such a distinction that for weeks friends would drop in to felicitate me. I was not yet aware that it was all Fani's doing. I thanked everybody appropriately and then asked Fani in a whisper why I had been summoned by the Prince. Fani feigned ignorance. He added that I was worthy of the honour and had to 'arrive' there eventually. 'I was alone so far. With your arrival, I shall have some company and strength. Now I shall enjoy this,' he said. I looked around the room, which was decked up like a bride inside. It looked like a spruced up office because on one side there was an office table with an ornate table lamp and stationery on it. I was surprised to note that there was no other lamp except the table lamp and yet the room was full of light. Worth mentioning amongst the courtiers was one Nawab Ummak Jung. He was a noble of modest means who had inherited little except a vast number of cane chairs. They would be arranged symmetrically in his drawing room conveying the erroneous impression that half of the nobles of Hyderabad would be coming to pay their respects to him.

He was an ordinary versifier. Occasionally he could compose a passable couplet but he was so fond of reciting his compositions that he would not leave anyone alone. Whether it was his house, office, playground, or a wedding, this 'ancient mariner' would catch hold of a victim. He had employed an old poet whom he paid Rs 25 a month. The Nawab would set a verse and the meter in which the poem was to be written. The mercenary poet would complete the poem, which would then be recited by our friend as his own. Undoubtedly he had a terrific memory. He knew by heart thousands of ghazals. Whomsoever he visited was in for trouble.

The other worthy was Nawab Dhimmak Jung. Destiny had put him on a high pedestal but he was also bereft of the capacity to versify. He used to place an order with a well-known ghazal 'manufacturing' company and receive ghazals by VPP. Those poems he would then submit to Tabatabai (a well-known poet) for correction and improvement. Then he would recite them as his own and receive felicitations with apparent modesty. He had a quicksilver temperament.

Because of our common interest, I was quite informal with both of them. We used to visit each other often. But in this house of magic, they behaved as if I were a stranger. The usual warmth was missing and that hurt me. I was still nursing the hurt when the silk curtain in front of me rustled, and a distinguished presence appeared. All the courtiers rose as one and started bowing and salaaming. It was a new experience for me to bend so low and to raise my hand repeatedly in salutation. I do not think I acquitted myself well in this ridiculous exercise. I was still engaged in the mechanical movement of the court salaams when I heard an awe-inspiring voice: 'Dhimmak Jung, forgive me. I kept you waiting so long. I shall call you soon.' Dhimmak Jung replied with folded hands: 'My Lord, it is no problem. I was sitting here quite comfortably.'

By now, I had completed my seven salaams. When I straightened myself, there was no one in front of me. The Prince had gone back. The curtain was still rustling slightly. I caught only a glimpse of the Prince. Fani recited this couplet to me in a whisper.

Ham naa kehte the yeh tum se ai kaleem
Aankh bijli pe naa daali jaae gi

Did I not tell you O' Moses
You won't be able to face the Light!

The grave and majestic manner in which the Prince had spoken to Dhimmak Jung showed that it was no ordinary person made of mortal clay. The voice clearly belonged to a superman who seemed to have descended from heaven. This unnerved me because I was yet to face the charismatic person formally.

I am going into these details so that those who have not seen a court can get an idea of its formalities and customs. This was the last court and even that is no more. Now nothing is left except my description. What will posterity know about the glitter and manners of these courts?

The court to which destiny took me was unique and even the courts of the Nizam and his Crown Prince were of no account in front of it. This was the only court in the Deccan. First Josh, then Fani, and lastly I enjoyed being there so much that we were fully sated.

An old courtier who could not complete his seven salaams in time was still busy doing his gesticulation.

After some time, a delicate, fairy-like boy in full court dress announced loudly that Sarkar (the Prince) had come to the dining table and had summoned us. Everyone entered the dining room respectfully. I kept sitting where I was. A minute later the same boy came and said, 'Kindly come. Why didn't you come with the others?'

My voice failed me but I brought myself to say that I was not in court dress. He smiled at my reply and went inside. Presently he returned and said: 'Sarkar says you are exempted. Remove your cap and come in.'

After this incident, I have pondered unsuccessfully my nervousness that day and wondered why my tongue had failed me? Was it the solemnity of the court or its splendour which had imparted a stammer to my speech and a shudder to my frame?

I entered the dining room with downcast eyes, like a prisoner who is to be handed his sentence. The room was brilliantly lit but again the source of this light was not apparent.

The Prince sat at the head of the table with great pomp. As I faced him, I made seven salaams. He acknowledged them with a slight motion of the head. Then he spoke: 'Come and sit by Fani's side.' He was sitting on the third chair to the right of the Prince. The fourth chair was vacant. Before sitting down dutifully, I again made my salaams. The first course was a pistachio-coloured soup. The Prince was the first to begin. The rest followed. The dining table was very elegant and costly. So were the crockery and cutlery. The menu was excellent. The room was redolent with the aroma of musk and saffron. In the centre of the table, fresh fruit was kept in beautiful bowls in such abundance that the table looked like a fruit shop. If the Prince addressed anyone at the table, he would stop eating at once and dropping the knife and fork, would fold his hands for the duration. This behaviour of the courtiers was a lesson for me and I noted it carefully. The Prince would take one morsel and talk for ten minutes. The addressee would go on saying, 'Right, Sarkar; Yes My Lord,' with folded hands. Presently, the Prince would turn to someone else so that everybody got a chance to eat. Taking advantage of this, I observed the Prince discreetly. He looked handsome, delicate, gentle, and cultured. I could feel him also observing me closely.

Whenever his eyes fell on me, I would pretend to be busy eating. God knows what impression he formed about me but I decided that there was no harm in becoming a courtier of that sort of Prince.

Some distance from me there were about a dozen handsome fair attendants only to serve water. At a mere hint from any guest, they would fill his glass. I wondered where the Prince got hold of so many comely and dashing youth. I later learnt that it was the result of efforts of the Commissioner of Police.

How can I describe each dish? Each grain of rice in the *biryani* seemed to be filled with *ghee* (clarified butter). The last dish consisted of almonds and cream. Bowls, each containing about 3 kilos of cream, were placed one in front of each person. Another dish, similarly placed, contained almonds and pistachios. Those nuts were eaten with cream. The layer of cream was at least three to four fingers thick. A measure of its sublime taste can be gauged from the fact that the buffaloes whose milk was used to make this cream were fed on almonds and pistachios morning and evening. I counted eleven bowls of cream that evening. That day the famed cream of Lucknow which I had tasted earlier at the table of the nobles of Avadh fell in my estimation.

Dinner took an hour to finish. First, the gracious Prince washed his' hands. Then our hands were washed. Some of the courtiers were given a special paan (folded betel-leaf) and a costly cigarette each. I was one of the' favoured ones. After that, the Prince got up and we dispersed.

Fani then took me out of the Palace and said: 'Come; let us stroll a bit. After that we will have to face the rigour of the court.' Fani also advised me not to open up with any of the courtiers. 'They are all inimical to us,' he added. 'Beneath their show of friendship, there is stark enmity. Consider everyone here ill-disposed towards you.'

After about half an hour, Fani looked at his watch and suggested we go in. It was time for the court. This time Fani took me towards the left side of the Palace. Here too there were a number of chairs laid all over a gallery. Beyond the gallery was a spacious hall, which was brilliantly illuminated. We sat down in the gallery where others too had gathered. The Prince emerged at half past ten sharp. Everyone got up and started salaaming him. The Prince acknowledged them with a slight nod as he entered the hall. We all sat down again.

Ten minutes later, a voice called from the hall: 'Dhimmak Jung.'

Dhimmak Jung responded: 'Yes, Sire' and proceeded briskly towards the hall. He stood before the Prince and made his courtly salaams. He was asked to take his seat. Then Ummak Jung was called. He too made the seven salaams and disappeared into the hall. Fani's turn was fourth. He was asked to bring me along. We went in together. The Prince was sitting in the centre. On the sofa to the right were Ummak Jung and Dhimmak Jung. I got a seat by the side of Fani on the first sofa on the left. The cockiness of Ummak Jung and Dhimmak Jung was worth seeing. It was as if they were sitting in the empyrean. By the time everybody settled down, it was 11.00. On both sides, there were about 35–7 courtiers.

By that time I had taken in the hall and its contents. The furniture was very elegant. The legs of the sofas and chairs were made of silver. In the centre, at the head, was a chair on which sat the Prince. Between every two courtiers, there was a big silver spittoon, which was as clean and shining as if it had just been bought from a shop. A round teapoy was similarly arranged between every two courtiers. On these teapoys were freshly opened tins of 555-brand cigarettes. The walls were adorned with exquisitely beautiful paintings.

The carpet in the hall was, I gathered, bought from Europe for Rs 7000. Costly silken curtains, matching with the walls, hung at every door. To the left of the Prince, there was a round teapoy, which shone like glass. On that were placed a very elegant timepiece and a beautiful glass along with a comb. Two big ceiling fans slowly circulated in the hall. There was really no need for them since it was winter. When the air disturbed the Prince's hair, he would adjust it with the comb. Whenever he did so, a servant would rush to him with a basin of water, a *lota* (a small metal mug), and a cake of soap. The Prince would wash his hands and then wipe them on a hand towel. That towel was then thrown onto a heap of soiled clothes. Thus in one night about a dozen towels would be discarded. I was awestruck at this height of refinement.

In short, there was such refinement in everything there and such an abundance of luxuries as I had not seen even during big celebrations in the courts of the rajas and maharajas of Avadh. Scenes from the Arabian Nights seemed to the brought alive in that court.

The lighting arrangement was a case in point. The hall was so well illuminated that even a needle on the floor could not escape attention. But so wonderful was the arrangement that there was no glare from the lamps, all of which faced upwards towards the ceiling. An exquisite corner-piece adorned each of the four corners of the ceiling. The Prince's beautiful face shone in this light like a full moon. Such was the awe inspired by this august presence that no one dared to look straight at him.

On the left side, I noticed a fair and delicate boy amongst the courtiers. Fani whispered to me that he was a Hindu boy and was an excellent dancer.

Presently we would witness his mastery of the art. By this time, everything was ready. The Prince called the boy up who salaamed and went and occupied a chair exactly opposite that of the Prince on the far side of the hall where there was a wooden platform covered with a beautiful carpet. On the right of the boy sat Moiz and on the left Bindu. The latter was a tabla[1] player and was a master of his art. A harmonium was placed in front of Moiz. At a signal, the music started and the boy began his dance. Fani whispered to me that they were all educated and had learnt to play the instruments as a hobby.

That handsome boy was the cynosure of all eyes in the hall. The Prince encouraged him by praising him off and on. Ummak Jung and Dhimmak Jung followed him vociferously jumping from their seats in their enthusiasm. This spectacle was no less amusing than the dance itself. Perhaps Fani and I were the only ones in the gathering who did not loudly express our appreciation. The dancer was behaving like a beloved exhibiting her coquetry in public. After dancing for about three quarters of an hour, the boy was dripping with sweat. The Prince thereupon signalled to him to stop. Everyone started showering the boy with praise, the Prince more so than anybody else. The boy salaamed in acknowledgement, got down from the platform, and took his seat.

A beautiful stand was then placed in front of Moiz. On that was placed a manuscript of a collection of the Prince's poems. The orchestra started playing again. Najm got up from his seat opposite ours and sat by my side. He whispered to me: 'Now the mushaira starts. Do not be restrained. Praise the compositions of the Prince as much as you can.' I nodded to reassure him. Then, to the accompaniment of the harmonium and the tabla, Moiz began to recite one of the Prince's poems. On the opening hemistich itself, Fani uttered a loud '*tauba*' (excellent) and slapped his thigh vigorously, swaying as if stung by a scorpion. The second line brought the roof down. Ummak Jung and Dhimmak Jung together uttered an ear-splitting '*Subhan Allah*' (God be praised). Both got up from their seats. With folded hands, Ummak Jung uttered effusively: 'The line has no parallel.' Dhimmak Jung in similar vein pronounced: 'It is an invaluable addition to Urdu literature, Huzur.' Fani too joined in with his praise: 'It is not the opening of a poem; it is the rising of sun!'

In short, everybody tried to excel each other in praise. Each tried to reach the very height of sycophancy. I looked on bewildered at the crazed courtiers, particularly at Ummak Jung and Dhimmak Jung who seemed to be so deranged that I feared they would soon tear off their clothes and rush out into the dark. Fani too seemed so delirious with admiration that I was afraid that his wild gestures may hit me. Because of this exuberance, there were repeated encores for the very first couplet. The praise was unending. Someone said that the soul of Mir (a celebrated Urdu poet of the eighteenth century) must have gone into a trance. Another said Souda (another famed poet of the eighteenth century) must have sat up in his grave. One courtier declared: 'Such felicity can't be humanly acquired.' Another added: 'Indeed it is a divine gift.'

I was completely unprepared for the outpouring of sycophancy although I was familiar with kings and their courts. But it must be said that I have heard few singers with a voice better than Moiz, so sweet and bewitching was it and so perfectly modulated. It was magic. Finally, the pandemonium died down. The two Nawabs regained their composure. Moiz then proceeded. It so happened that at that time Dhimmak Jung had taken his costly cigar from his mouth and was holding it between his fingers. He was holding himself in readiness to praise the second couplet. But Ummak Jung got the better of him and even before the completion of the couplet, shouted 'Subhan Allah', throwing out his arms wildly. His hand hit Dhimmak Jung's hand and caused the cigar to fall into the spittoon. Dhimmak Jung's look of pathetic rage for a moment made me forget that I was in the court of the Prince and I broke into a guffaw. Luckily in the general bedlam, no one took notice, otherwise I might have been thrown out.

Moiz went on singing ghazal after ghazal. I sat entranced by the music and the poetry. Every couplet was worthy of praise. But I could never match the laudatory fervour of the other courtiers. Singing the fifth or sixth ghazal, Moiz came to this couplet:

> *Waide kaa bhi iqraar hai aane se bhi inkaar*
> *Waide hi se tum apne mukar kyon nahin jaate?*[2]

> You promise—and yet refuse to come.
> Why don't you go back on your word?

Moiz had hardly finished the first half of the second hemstitch that Shyam of Agra who was a little high that evening completed it incorrectly with *'guzar kyon nahin jaate'.*

He then proceeded to praise the line. With folded hands, he exclaimed exuberantly: 'Highness, what a couplet! One cannot praise it enough.' And repeating his construction, he continued: 'Subhan Allah, Subhan Allah. What a meter, my Master! It has no equal!' The Prince started laughing at this impertinence. He asked me to correct him. I repeated the correct words loudly. But in that state of inebriation, Shyam heard me wrong, repeated the incorrect line aloud, and continued praising it. 'Subhan Allah, Subhan Allah, Sire, this slave has never heard such expressive lines before.' Now the courtiers also joined the Prince in laughing. Then the Prince ordered that Shyam needed some fresh air and he be taken out. The orchestra came to a sudden stop. Two courtiers took hold of Shyam and handed him over to the servants.

The Prince ordered coffee. I looked at the watch. It was 1.00 in the morning. Fani pulled out his pocket box and took a paan out of it. Dhimmak Jung lighted his second cigar. The fairy-faced attendants placed a cup and saucer first before the Prince and then before each one of us. The crockery was exquisite. One servant put two cubes of sugar in my cup. The coffee was delicious. The milk again came from the buffaloes that were fed on almonds and pistachios. After finishing his coffee, the Prince went inside. Fani spread his feet on the sofa. I also relaxed. Fani advised me also to stretch myself. After that break of half an hour the second sitting would start which would last till 3.00 in the morning.

Each one utilized this interval in his own way. Ummak Jung and Dhimmak Jung rushed towards the toilet. Some washed their faces to keep the sleep away. Moiz and Bindu went to another room and lay down. The handsome youngster who had danced so well combed his hair. I took out a cigarette. Fani meanwhile kept talking to me softly.

The Prince returned after about forty-five minutes. He had had a wash. The courtiers repeated the exercise of seven salaams. Moiz and Bindu were sent for. The orchestra started playing and the second session began.

Again every couplet of the Prince's poems produced a tumult with every courtier trying to outdo the other in loud and fulsome praise. Moiz was singing a prelude to a song. I noticed a distinguished European also in this gathering. He was sitting still as a picture on a chair in the row opposite mine, watching the breast-beating and dress-tearing antics of the two Nawabs in silent wonder. Fani told me that he was the staff surgeon. It was his duty to be present at night. He got a salary of Rs 1500 per month. In the morning, when the Prince retired for rest, his duty ended.

By the time three ghazals had been recited, it was 3.00 in the morning. Then, at a signal from the Prince, the orchestra stopped. Moiz and Bindu got down from the platform and took their seats. The Prince then asked for his medicine. An attendant brought a small bottle and placed it before the Prince. He took two tablets out of it and swallowed them. Two tablets were given to Najm. He too swallowed them with water.

The Prince then stood up. He ordered: 'Fani, go and take some rest now. Drop Sidney at his place.' 'Very well, Sarkar', replied Fani. I also bade the Prince farewell. He said '*Khuda Hafiz*' and turned towards his bedroom. The courtiers responded with 'Khuda Hafiz' in turn. Fani and I lit our cigarettes and shook hands with Ummak Jung and Dhimmak Jung by way of farewell. As I stepped into the courtyard from the hall I saw scores of official cars. The chauffeurs were sleeping in them. The servants woke them up. The guests started mounting their cars. Fani and I got into the third or fourth car. When the car started, I heaved a sigh of relief.

I asked Fani if Najm had gone by some other car. Fani laughed and replied: 'We are honorary courtiers and so got off early. Najm is a paid courtier. He is on duty till 6.00.' I said, 'The Prince must have gone to sleep. What would then Najm be doing then?' Fani replied that His Highness would be lying under a mosquito net. All the paid courtiers would sit around him on chairs and chat with him. At 6.00, the Prince would go to sleep. Only then would they be able to go home. I should mention here that Najm Afandi was the poetry instructor of the Prince and was paid for the job. Like Fani, his courtiership was also 'honorary'. But because of his closeness to the Prince, he was obliged to shadow him all the time.

I prayed to God to save me from such proximity. I then enquired about the medicine which the Prince and Najm had taken. Were teacher and student suffering from the same disease? Fani laughed heartily and said, 'You want to learn all the secrets of the court in one night? Here are layers on layers of mysteries. I have been engaged in this labour for ten years and yet have not been able to unravel all the mysteries. The tablets which the Prince took are from Germany. They are called finadome. They are sleeping pills. But they are so potent that anyone taking a pill for the first time is knocked out for twenty-four hours. Nothing can wake him up.' I said in alarm, 'But the Prince took two pills and gave the same dose to Najm also'. Fani said that the Prince had developed a measure of immunity due to prolonged use. He took two pills at 3.00 a.m. and was able to sleep only at 6.00 a.m. The same was true of Najm. He too could not sleep without them.

I felt a shudder run through my frame on hearing this and asked no further questions. In a short while, we reached our house. I said goodbye to Fani and got down from the car. As I lay on the bed, I looked at the watch. It was exactly 4.00 a.m. I fell asleep by half past four and got up only at 10.00 a.m.

The Second Night at the Court

HAVING BEEN SUBJECTED to the rigours of court etiquette and the night-long vigil, every limb of my body was aching when I woke up. Fortunately, it was a holiday. I got up leisurely, had my bath, changed, and sat down for my breakfast. By then, it was 11.00 a.m. The hangover of the previous night pushed me towards sleep again but I resisted. I drew some energy by sipping two cups of tea. Putting the paan-box in my pocket, I sent for a carriage and proceeded towards the Chowk (a public square with different kinds of shops near the Charminar). I bought a beautiful bagloos from a silversmith. Then I found a shop where I ordered a dove-coloured dastar. That was the colour of the dastar used at the Prince's court. By the time I finished with this it was 2.00 in the afternoon. Reaching home at half past two, I had my lunch and slept for a long time. At dusk, a car from the garage of the Prince pulled up in front of my house. The chauffeur informed me that I had been summoned and that I should be ready by 7.30 p.m. He would collect Fani and then come to pick me up.

I got ready hurriedly. The car came to my house exactly at the appointed time. Fani was very pleased to see me in formal dress. We went together to the Hill Fort Palace. I was not as nervous as on the previous evening but still felt some trepidation. I noticed three new and distinguished faces at the dining table that day. During dinner, the Prince talked mostly to them. This gave me a good opportunity to observe him without being noticed myself.

Amongst the newcomers was a handsome old gentleman whose demeanour betrayed his noble ancestry. The Prince addressed him as 'Piya'. The second person was dark in complexion and lacked the noble bearing of the first. Without his costly dress, he would have passed for an ordinary clerk. The third guest seemed to be around 80. Though he was not expensively dressed, his noble extraction and scholarship were evident from the way he behaved and talked. The Prince called him 'Carew'.

As usual, dinner lasted one hour. Piya and Carew instead of Ummak Jung and Dhimmak Jung occupied the first sofa that evening. Ummak and Dhimmak sat on the second sofa. By the side of the Prince's seat in the centre sat the dark-complexioned guest. In front of him stood a very beautiful round teapoy on which was placed a shining silver paan-box. He made a paan, got up, and presented it very respectfully to the Prince. After that, he took one himself. When everyone had settled down, the Prince addressed me and asked: 'Sidq, have you brought your copy-book of poems?' 'No, Sarkar,' I stood up and replied with folded hands, 'I seldom carry that.'

Fani stood up and submitted: 'My Lord, he does not need his book. Whatever he had written since his childhood is stored in his memory and he can recite it for months if Your Grace would deign to listen to it. Not only that. He also remembers by heart the entire works of the most famous poets.'

The Prince looked at me with astonishment and asked me to take a seat between Piya and Carew. I got up, made seven courtly bows and went and sat between the two new guests.

The Prince then pointed towards the dark gentleman by his side and said to me, 'He is our uncle, Nawab Qudrat Nawaz Jung. Apart from being a landlord, he is also the Military Secretary in the government.' I got up and greeted him with bows. He also got up and returned my greetings. Then referring to his introduction by the Prince, he said with folded hands: 'My Lord you are very kind to your servants. I am only a humble slave of yours.'

The Prince once again turned to me: 'On your left,' he said, 'is Nawab Nasir-ud-Dowla who was a particularly close friend and a companion of my late grandfather. He has a noble lineage. I call him "Piya".' I rose and made the customary bows to him. He also got up and returned my salutation with a smile. 'On your right,' added the Prince, 'is Qari Suleiman who was a tutor of my brother and I in our childhood. I am very attached to him and call him Carew out of affection.' After this introduction, he said, 'Right. Now you recite that ghazal of yours which made me so restless for such a long time. Fani, tell him of that night's incident when you recited his couplet and what effect it had on me.'

Fani turned to me and said, 'Sidq, it was the following couplet':

> '*Us ke lutfe-aam ko ghairat nahin karti qabool*
> *Aur main kambahkt lutfe-khaas ke kaabil nahin.*'

'I can't describe,' continued Fani, 'the spell it cast on His Honour. For about half-an-hour he made me repeat this couplet. He would just not be sated. He asked scores of questions about you. I told him whatever I knew.'

Now I understood the background. I was there because of Fani's mischief!

Then the Prince said to Fani, 'Tell him how many times I made you recite this couplet?'

'At least nine times,' replied Fani.

The Prince then observed: 'Piya, a master has no horns or tail. Whoever can compose such a perfect couplet is a master.' Piya responded with folded hands: 'Your remark is absolutely correct, Sire.' Then he added, 'What an insightful observation!' Turning to me, he added, 'Sidq Sahib, congratulations. The Sarkar has conferred the honour of a master on you. It is a matter of great pride.' I got up and made my obeisance first to the Prince and then to Piya. Thereupon I was asked to recite that ghazal.

I recited the opening couplet.[1]

The Prince exclaimed graciously: 'Very good.' Fani, Piya, Carew, Qudrat Jung all praised it. Ummak Jung and Dhimmak Jung also commended it. On the second couplet the Prince remarked: 'Piya, how simple and effective his poetry is!' Piya replied, 'Your Honour, it reminds me of Dagh.'

Then turning to me, he said, 'What a piece!' I got up and offered my thankful salaams first to the Prince, then to Piya. The Prince observed, 'Sidq, it is not an easy thing to elicit praise from Piya. He has heard Dagh recite before his Late Highness.'[2]

I bowed my head. I recited the couplet:

> *Mere dushman wasl se maayoos hon, ai gham gusaar*
> *Us ki ghaflat hi to kehti hai keh who ghaafil nahin.*

> My enemies despair of her favours
> Her oversight shows that she cares.

The Prince exclaimed spontaneously: 'Very beautiful.' Piya and Fani acclaimed it in superlatives. Piya folded his hands and said to the Prince: 'It is an outcome of love. Your slave knows that no one other than a person who has been smitten can write such poetry.' The Prince started laughing. Piya was insistent. He besought the Prince to order an investigation to find out the truth. 'If he is not in love, Your Lordship may spit on my face,' he said. Everybody laughed at this.

The Prince said: 'It is my conviction that to attempt to write poetry without the experience of love is mere raving.' Fani seconded him with folded hands: 'Well said, Sire. There is no taste or savour in poetry without love.' Piya made the profound observation that far from writing poetry, he who had not been in love could not even understand it. Since I had to acknowledge every expression of praise by standing and raising my right hand repeatedly in salutation, the muscles of my arm and back started aching, especially because of the seven floor salaams which I had to make each time to the Prince. Recitation took the life out of me that evening. To cut a long story short, I had to recite five poems one after another that night. And every couplet had to be recited at least twice, some even thrice. By the time the proceedings ended, I was completely exhausted.

Then the Prince remarked, 'Piya, it is very good poetry. Apart from that, I have observed Sidq closely. In every respect is he worthy of admittance into my court.' On this announcement, I got up and went through the motions of seven floor salaams again. Nawab Qudrat Nawaz Jung got up from his seat and walked up to me. He shook my hand and congratulated me saying that His Lordship had heard as many as five poems from me. Such an honour had not yet been conferred on anyone else. Then, lowering his voice to a whisper, he told me, 'Mr Sidq, it is a great court!'

I thanked him appropriately.

Dhimmak Jung addressed the Prince with folded hands: 'Because of this gesture of My Lord, I will now have the privilege of meeting Sidq every day.' Ummak Jung joined him. But I could not forget their look of disdain at our first meeting. I decided to conceal my true feelings and thanked them for their kind words.

Truth to tell, it was their scorn that made me determined to become a courtier. Otherwise, I would somehow have broken free of the trap laid for me by Fani. But now I had become interested in becoming firmly established in the court. Where then was the question of my escaping? Moreover, the Prince had announced my appointment himself!

On a signal from the Prince, Moiz and Bindu ascended the dais. The tabla began to be tapped. In the terminology of the Hill Fort, the mushaira had started. The courtiers praised the compositions of the Prince sky high and that night too passed in tumult and uproar. Fani and I were let off at 3.00 in the morning. Nawab Qudrat Jung, Piya, and Carew were also relieved. Coming out of the Palace, they shook my hand warmly and expressed their pleasure at that day's meeting. I thanked each one individually.

After I got free of them, the moon-faced dancer of the previous night stepped forward, shook my hand, and praised my poems. He said that my poems had made him restless and requested me to write them down for him. I agreed. He insisted that I should bring them the next day and entreated me not to break my promise. Fani told him I dared not do that. Then I got into the car with Fani. On the way back, Fani also congratulated me and said that the Prince had liked me, but he wanted to hear from me my opinion of the court. 'Did you enjoy these two nights or did you stay out of compulsion? What are your future plans?'

I told him that I felt privileged to belong to such a court, presided over by such a handsome and genial prince and amongst courtiers who were either from noble families or were high officials or men of letters or other accomplishments. My salary from the government, moreover, sufficed for my livelihood and I had no need of any financial favour from the Prince. The only problem was keeping awake at night. After the nightlong vigil, how was one to discharge one's duties the next day? Fani replied: 'Indeed that is a problem, but we will ponder over it later. Right now I wanted to hear that you have accepted and, God be praised, I have heard it.' Then he added that hitherto he had felt alone and threatened at the court like a tongue in the midst of thirty-two teeth. Now he felt reassured by my presence. He then proceeded to warn me: 'Remember one thing. Never consider any courtier your friend. None of them is trustworthy. Treat them with apparent friendship; but be on your guard.' I said that would be very difficult. Fani replied that it was nothing. 'Every flower is surrounded by thorns, but still flowers are plucked by intelligent people. Of course if anyone is careless, he is bound to be hurt.'

The two nights described here belong to 1936.

From then on, I became very busy. Every night I had dinner with the Prince without fail, then lauded the 'official' poetry till 3.00 in the morning, returned home at 4.00, and then went to sleep at a time when one should wake up. Getting up at 9.00 a.m., I got ready in great haste, looked into the accounts of the hostel between 4.00 and 6.00 in the evening, gave

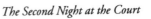

instructions to the accountant, listened to the complaints of the boarders and disposed of them, and then got ready for the nocturnal court. That became my routine.

Fani had no other work at that time except to attend court. Being on sick leave from the school, he was master of his time, He continued to get Rs 200 from the Maharaja every month. The sick-leave pay came about once a year. He saw through the intervening period by getting loans. However, the interest due to moneylenders kept mounting.

Incidentally, my wife had passed away the previous year, that is in 1935. I was thus alone and so did not have to explain my absence during the night to anybody. Fani was old and his wife was not young either. So he did not have any conjugal obligation which would stand in the way of his courtiership. Rather than lie alone at night at home, it was better to enjoy the merriment at the Palace.

Earlier I had spent some years in the company of Sir Syed Abu Jaffer of Pir Pur in Avadh (UP), and with the late Prince of Bhopal, Habeebullah Khan. I therefore considered myself to be quite adept at court manners. But observing Piya (Nawab Nasir-ud-Dowla) at the court of the Prince of Hyderabad, I was soon disabused of my notion.

Whatever the subject of discussion at the court, Piya could not refrain from participating. And he did it so expertly that everyone was appreciative. Watching him perform there, I came to learn that the principal function of a courtier was to ensure that the Prince never felt bored or became melancholy. It was not an easy job. Piya had to remember by heart thousands of anecdotes and jokes, which he narrated in an inimitable style. And we all shared the enjoyment of the Prince.

But Piya himself became the stuff of anecdotes once in this way. Though Piya had gone all over the country in the company of the sixth Nizam, he had had no occasion to travel out of India. Such an opportunity came his way in old age when he accompanied the Prince on a pilgrimage to the holy places of Islam. In India, long gowns are associated with dervishes or religious people and Piya believed that only the learned and pious wore such dresses. The second day after their arrival in Baghdad, a servant brought in a visiting card. The visitor was a young Egyptian on whose fair and pink face grew an attractive black beard. Seeing his long gown and turban and struck by his beauty and grace, Piya took his hands and touched them with his eyes to show his respect. Greeting him thus, he sat down deferentially. The visitor talked to the Prince for sometime in French and when he was departing, Piya bade him with farewell excessive deference.

After he had gone, Piya asked the Prince who the visitor was. 'Was he a religious scholar or a keeper of a shrine? What a radiant face! Your slave felt truly lifted,' Piya declared warmly. The Prince replied coolly: 'He came on business. He requested me to spare an hour and promised to show me such stunners that I would forget the belles of India.'

Piya was startled. 'My God,' he exclaimed with disbelief, 'So he was a pimp. Forgive me, My God.' The Prince roared with laughter. Piya kept slapping his face and vowing repentance. Once bitten, twice shy, for the rest of the trip, Piya did not talk even to genuinely pious people. Whenever this incident was mentioned in the court, Piya used to say, 'God is pure and merciful. I committed this sin in ignorance. He will probably excuse me.' Piya was good and gentle and an interesting noble and courtier. May God pardon him!

We were still steeped in the luxuries of the court when the month of fasting came. On the auspicious occasion of Eid, those attached to the Prince got sherwanis (long buttoned-up coats) as presents from him. None—from the highest to the lowest—was ignored. Of course, there was a classification. Courtiers got sherwani lengths worth Rs 250 while servants got pieces worth Rs 100 each. The famous tailor of Secunderabad, John Burton, stitched these sherwanis. The evening of Eid thus presented a spectacle worth watching.

The procedure was that a few days before the great feast, the Prince, accompanied by three or four paid courtiers, would visit the Burton shop at about 10.00 in the morning. Burton extended a royal welcome to the party. Chairs would be spread out in that part of the shop where sherwani rolls were kept. All the while Burton himself would remain standing in front of the Prince with folded hands. The shop assistants would keep spreading the rolls before the Prince. After seeing a number of pieces, he would select one for a particular courtier. The measurements of all the courtiers were recorded in the shop. A slip carrying the name of the recipient was pinned to the selected piece and it was separated from the rest. All the pieces were specially manufactured in France and were usually of a 2-m length only so that each sherwani was unique. Every piece of cloth had buttons to match it.

Thus the whole day was spent in selecting sherwani lengths. In the language of the court, it was called 'amusing the fast'. So long as the Prince stayed in the shop, no one else could enter it. Only European ladies with whom the Prince was on informal terms were excluded from this ban. But they were very few, generally the wives of top British military officers.

The long days of the month of fasting were thus whiled away. During that month, no mushaira was held. After dinner, there would be chit-chat till 2.00 in the morning. Generally, religious topics were discussed. In between, women would also crop up in the discussion. A day before Eid, dancers specially invited from Delhi, Agra, Lucknow, and Bombay would start arriving. Shyam was in charge of supplies. During this period, Shyam's pomposity was worth viewing. Wearing a rust-coloured headdress and a belt on his sherwani, he would strut around looking after his guests and showing greater pride in his assignment than the keeper of a religious shrine.

The Night of Eid

THE PRINCE SPENT RECKLESSLY on dancing girls. Let me describe the occasion, during my seven years of courtiership, when I saw an agent being dispatched to collect them.

It was the 27th day of the month of Ramadan. Fani and I were sitting at our respective places in the court. Suddenly an agent called Siddiqui arrived, made the Darbari floor salaams, and stood aside. He was paid Rs 50 per month by the Prince, and he ate with him. The Prince spoke to him: 'You are going to Bombay by the morning train.' Siddiqui bowed his head in acquiescence. The Prince added, 'I have given the necessary orders. You take the required amount from so and so. I have sanctioned Rs 7000 for the journey. Travel first-class, stay in a first-class hotel in Bombay, and confirm the deal with the best. If the amount you are taking with you is not sufficient, send me a telegram and I will send you more money. But remember one thing. From the moment the party reaches the railway platform to travel to Hyderabad, they are our guests. From then on, arrange for their hospitality as befits our status. Don't worry about money.' Siddiqui folded his hands and submitted, 'This servant of Your Lordship shall always keep your dignity and prestige in mind at every step, Sarkar.'

The Prince then addressed Piya, 'What do you say, Piya? Shouldn't 'they be our guests once they reach the platform?' Piya replied with folded hands, 'Quite right, Sir. They should be treated on a scale appropriate to the honoured guests of an exalted Prince.'

The Prince looked at Siddiqui as if to ascertain whether he had heard what had been said. Siddiqui was probably making a mental calculation that out of Rs 7000, he could appropriate at least Rs 5000. He did not say anything. He just bowed his head with folded hands.

Siddiqui was an ordinary person. He would hardly ever have travelled inter-class (a class between the second and third in the railways, now abolished) on his own. But now he was being asked to travel first. He got this honour for having sold his soul? Here was Siddiqui having a good time. He could scribble any amount on a piece of paper. Was there no one to check him? Who would dare to? And there was Fani in dire need with debts piling up. But such was the irony of court life: there was plenty of money to be made by the dishonourable, those who clung to their honour were likely to earn little other than respect.

Another agent was one Farooqui. He was an MA. The third agent was a Parsi. He stayed permanently in Bombay. He used to be given written orders. He would always come with a 'gift' for the Prince. His standing in the court was far above that of Siddiqui or Farooqui. When I first saw him, from the informal way in which he behaved with the Prince, I took him to be a ruler or a prince of some state. Luckily the Prince himself introduced him to me. He made so much money on just one order as Siddiqui and Farooqui couldn't hope to acquire in ten trips.

The fourth agent was one of our colleagues at the court. Having seen that a life of honesty did not pay, he had turned into a procurer for the sake of his family.

Apart from these permanent agents, some others like Shyam and Pattan also engaged off and on in this profitable activity, but these people could not achieve the level of prosperity of Siddiqui and Farooqui. They did sell their souls, but did not get the world. As someone has said:

> *Na khudaa hi milaa naa wasaal-e-sanam*
> *Naa idhar ke rahe naa udhar ke hue*

> They got neither God, nor the beloved
> They were neither here, nor there.

The groups of entertainers would start descending at Nampally (the main railway station of Hyderabad) from the morning of Eid. Shyam, in his formal dress of belted sherwani and dastar, would receive each troupe. He was above 50, but would make his bows to the prima donna and meet each member of her entourage with youthful elan.

Then he would take each group to the bungalow allocated to them. On that day, as he put it himself, he did not have time even to die. He would join each group at mealtimes and would be more respectful to the dancer and singer than one would be to one's own mother.

On the night of Eid, when I arrived at the Hill Fort Palace with Fani, used as I had become to its daily resplendence, I was astonished to see its embellishment on this special occasion. Moreover, in red and green sherwanis, even the handsome servants looked like nobles.

While we were still admiring the beauty of the Palace and its attendants, there appeared the handsome dancer boy. On seeing me, he smiled and put his right hand on his heart by way of salutation. That was how we greeted each other in court. I returned his greetings. The scent of his perfume pervaded the room. Fani started praising it. I recited an appropriate couplet, which he liked very much. He said I seemed to be in top form. I replied that one was automatically elevated to new heights upon seeing the added beauty of the Palace on the special occasion.

The courtiers were there in full force that day. In addition, scores of nobles had come to present their nazar.[1]

Everyone was dressed in costly, attractive sherwanis and the whole Palace presented a festive atmosphere such as I had never seen before. Hundreds of government officials were also lined up to make their presentations.

The Prince took quite some time to come out. The nobles were the first to make their offerings. Officers of the government followed them. The Prince would touch each nazar lightly with his hand; then a servant would collect it and the presenter of the nazar would make his courtly bow and walk backwards bowing all the while.

The crowd thinned after some time. After the outsiders had finished, the turn of the courtier came. The Prince himself accepted Fani's nazar and mine. That was a great honour. We did seven floor salaams to express our gratitude.

The nazar ceremony took a long time. The Prince came to the dining table at 10.00. About seventy-five persons were at the special dinner. As usual, there were two *chapattis*[2] each in front of Fani and me. All the people of Hyderabad, rich or poor, ate toast or *paratha*[3] only at breakfast. For the other meals—lunch or dinner—they ate only rice, whether plain boiled or a special biryani. It was rice country and so people liked to eat rice. As a special consideration for people like us from 'India', chapattis were specially provided. It was not worthwhile making the chapattis in the Prince's kitchen. They were, therefore, specially made at a restaurant in Nampally, the owner of which was also a 'Hindustani' like us.

At the end of the meal, a servant brought five round wafers of *sohan halwa* (an Indian sweet) not less than 20 kg each in weight. The Prince said to Fani, 'It is a delicacy from your country—from Lucknow. So, you and Sidq will relish it.' Saying this, he placed one cake of the sweet each in our respective plates. We got up and made the customary obeisance to acknowledge the special favour. The Prince then ordered that one piece each be given to all the guests. That evening everyone ate sohan halwa with the special cream of Hill Fort. No one looked at the almond pudding.

Amongst the guests for the dinner, there were about ten officials. They had no special relationship with the Prince. I will mention only one of them. His name was Kamaluddin and he sported the poetic pen-name of 'Kammo'.[4] He was the Superintendent of the Public Gardens. Hundreds of gardeners—male and female—worked under him. He was a man of amorous disposition known to fool around with young and comely female gardeners. In the time he had to spare from such pursuits, he turned to versification. He had a published volume to his credit. Since his work is no longer available due to public indifference, I present a sample:

> *Dil doodh ko bechain naa makhan ke liye hai*
> *Golan se savaa, dukhtar-e-golan ke liye hai*

> My heart pines neither for milk nor butter
> More than the gardener, I fancy her daughter.

Kamaluddin had a warped sense of duty and work ethic as the following anecdote demonstraters. One evening he was standing in his verandah. It was raining heavily. He summoned the head gardener and asked him why the gardeners were not watering the plants. The latter replied that it was raining. Kamaluddin thundered: 'Never mind the rain. Let them take umbrellas and water the plants. Duty is duty. I won't let them earn their bread without work.' Since that day the gardeners had to water the plants even during the rainy season with umbrellas on their heads!

Curiosity motivated both the Princes to grant Kamaluddin an audience. The simpleton provided enough amusement for the Prince of Berar to start inviting him for lunch and the Junior Prince for dinner. How Kammo Mian earned his keep, God alone knows. But his lunch and dinner were taken care of for the rest of his life. Because of the daily feasting, he started putting on weight. He became so fat, he could hardly walk. On that particular Eid night, he heaved himself up with difficulty. The party was at its height with music and dance. Someone from Agra was dancing. Behind the singer were ranged the instrumentalists. A tipsy Kammo stamped on the feet of one of them. His victim uttered a shrill cry of pain. The Prince pulled him up and observed harshly: 'Kammo, be careful. You are like the proverbial elephant which mauled its own forces.' The courtiers started tittering at this remark. I folded my hands and said: 'Sire, this metaphor of "own forces" is great.' At this the Prince also laughed and said, 'Of course these people are from amongst his offspring.' Kammo felt the snub and sat down.

A dozen singing women had been arranged for the night of Eid. Some of them were young, some past their prime. But each one was an expert in her trade. The Prince wanted all of them to be present at the gathering. He therefore suggested that one of them should sing from the dais while others should sit along with the courtiers. A 30-year old beauty was asked to sit near Fani. A 20-year old was parked next to me. Fani thanked the Prince by making seven salaams but was somewhat embarrassed at this special favour. The Prince asked me whether I was satisfied with my partner. I said I believed in fate. One got what one was fated to, 'I bow before my fate, Sire.'

The other singers were allocated to the special courtiers. Some matrons were sent over to give company to the older courtiers. Piya and Carew too were not overlooked in this dispensation. At a signal, an old hag reached the side of a reluctant and bashful Carew. Such light practical jokes enhanced the merriment of Eid.

Only one middle-aged singer of ample proportions was left sitting on the carpet. The Prince was in a fix about how to dispose of her. I suggested respectfully that she should be 'dispensed' suitably. The Prince asked for my suggestion. I winked towards Dhimmak Jung. The latter retorted that it would be appropriate if I seated her on my other side. The Prince enjoyed this exchange. He got up laughing, took hold of one plump arm and seated her by Dhimmak Jung's side who simply smiled submissively.

Then the tabla began to be beaten and the guest artistes started exhibiting their skills. All of them had received gifts of Eid suits from the Prince. Each singer was given a *sari* worth a thousand rupees with a blouse to match, and her accompanists got sherwanis worth a hundred rupees each. Dame luck had smiled on them. Wearing those sherwanis, they were beside themselves with joy. No one noticed the passage of time that night. Only when the morning azan[5] was heard did the music and dance come to a halt. The courtiers were asked to have a wash so that after breakfast they could go home. So fatigued was I with the nightlong entertainment that the breakfast from the royal kitchen tasted as bitter as a plateful of *neem* (margosa) leaves.

In this merry heedless way, time flew by as on wings. Suddenly, Fani's wife was taken ill. He needed money urgently for her treatment. He had to resort to more loans from moneylenders. With time, his wife's condition grew worse. Within a year, she was completely bedridden. The physicians diagnosed cancer. The treatment required a considerable amount of money, which Fani had no means of laying his hands on. He started using cheap medicine. Feroz Ali Khan, Fani's younger son, started bringing medicines from the government hospitals while Fani continued to attend the court. Occasionally, the Prince would enquire about Fani's wife's health. Fani would reply that she was in a bad way and he did not know whether he would find her alive on his return home. That would be the end of the topic. The month of Muharram[6] arrived and all offices and schools were closed for twelve days. On the seventh day of the month, I had just finished my bath when Shyam came and informed me that Fani's wife had expired the previous night. I put on my sherwani and reached Fani's house, which was five minutes' walk from mine.

When we reached the graveyard, I counted the number of mourners present. There were, in all, twenty-three persons including Fani and his two sons. Surprised at this thin attendance, I asked Fani whether he had not informed his friends and well-wishers. Fani replied, 'Of course, I had the Maharaja, the Prince, Ummak Jung, and Dhimmak Jung informed on the phone. What can I do if they don't care?'

I realized suddenly that Fani had an unfortunate weakness for the rich and titled. The latter, however, cared little for him beyond applauding his poetry at formal or informal gatherings. However, it was hardly the occasion to talk to him about it so I kept quiet. Of the long list of titled and decorated officials that Fani informed of his wife's death, only one, Nawab Nisar Yar Jung 'Mizaj', came to offer his condolences. That too because he had retired from service and no longer had any special standing in the city.

Qazi Abdul Ghaffar,[7] meanwhile, arrived in his car. He helped Fani and his sons wash. He had brought food for half-a-dozen persons with him with which he fed the mourners. Fani had not even bothered to inform him about the death of his wife and yet the Qazi rendered him sincere help in his time of difficulty. But even this didn't serve to open Fani's eyes.

At least after that he could have removed the names of the dignitaries from his list of friends. Better still, he should have burnt that list. But more suffering was yet in store for Fani. He kept that list close to his heart.

Perhaps other inexperienced people could learn something from Fani's suffering and not be taken in by the spurious friendship of the rich and the mighty.

Three days later a petty messenger came to Fani on behalf of the Prince and offered his condolences in the following words: 'Sarkar says that he is sorry to learn of your wife's death.'

That afternoon a note from the Prime Minister, Maharaja Kishen Pershad, conveyed His Excellency's condolences. In the evening Dhimmak Jung came. He expressed his sorrow but his lack of sincerity was apparent. Ummak Jung did not feel the need even for such a formality. He must have thought that it would be enough to convey his sympathies at the next meeting at the Hill Fort.

None of the other worthies bothered even with the formality of a note. People of Fani's own class came to commiserate with him but they couldn't provide him solace. He was waiting for his fellow courtiers. Little did he know that they wouldn't bother to turn out even at his own death. The Maharaja, who truly respected men of letters, would have sent his ADC and Rs 500 for the obsequies, had he not been displeased with Fani at his prolonged absence from his court. Such courtesy was characteristic of him.

But other nobles thought that to merely praise and applaud literary men was enough for their survival. Though a number of them were a lot richer than the Maharaja, their wealth was frittered away on women. Neither destitution nor learning moved them to spend a pie but they would think nothing of burning thousands on empty pomp and show.

A very big noble of the Deccan who had 25–30 chickens for every meal was known to hold a court that was famous for its frivolity and grossness. The worth of his courtiers was judged by their ability to indulge in obscenities. He used to abuse others and exulted in being abused in turn. The sort of things uttered in his court are too disgraceful to be mentioned. The tragedy of the degenerate nobility of the Deccan was encapsulated in the fact that the goons who shared his company and his cup were spinning around in cars while men of letters like Fani and Yagana Changezi[8] were living in misery.

Hardly had Fani's wife been buried when Fani started attending the Hill Fort gatherings again. If anyone condoled with him, he would smile wanly and say: 'Our life reverts to its old course.' Now Fani was free. He would keep awake the whole night. During the day, he would take the medicine brought from the government dispensary to bolster his waning energy. At home, he ate abstemiously; at the royal dinner, he would observe no precaution.

As if this were not enough, some of his jealous friends, who by their passable versification considered themselves front-rank poets but had no standing in the literary world, conspired with the moneylenders to whom Fani owed money and instigated them to send Fani to jail for non-payment of debts. Succumbing to the pressure, some of the moneylenders joined forces and a number of suits were filed against Fani simultaneously. The rumour spread that Fani was about to be jailed. Qazi Abdul Ghaffar once again came to the rescue. He met Nawab Hosh Yar Jung on his own and they decided together to come to Fani's rescue. Thereafter the Qazi met each of Fani's creditors individually and told them that they only stood to lose by litigation. It was, therefore, advisable to come to a settlement.

For almost a month, he had to spend 2–3 hours daily with Fani's creditors to bring them round. In the end he liquidated all Fani's debts, amounting to over Rs 7000, with Hosh's help. Each creditor was paid about half his dues and they all fell in line because of the Qazi's efforts and Hosh's influence. And thus the one indignity that Fani was spared before his death was that of going to jail.

Meanwhile Fani's 'intimate' friends, lounging on their comfortable sofas in their mansions, did little more than express sorrow for Fani's misfortunes.

After the settlement of his debts, Hosh felt that Fani would be better off returning home. Hyderabad was not a city for men of letters. Hosh entrusted the job of persuading Fani to leave Hyderabad to Qazi Abdul Ghaffar. After a lot of discussion, Fani agreed to leave. He started packing his baggage and one evening, with a heavy and unwilling heart he left the house in which he was fated to die. His dear friends embraced him and bid him goodbye.

But by the time Fani reached Secunderabad railway station, the Grand Trunk Express, which he was to board, was steaming out of the platform.

Declining a Job

FANI TOOK HEART. He took the missing of the train as an omen that he should not leave Hyderabad. He felt he was fated to live there, suffer there, and die there. He had agreed to undertake the journey only because he had no arguments to counter Qazi Abdul Ghaffar's lucid and sincere arguments. Now he had an excuse. He had left the house unwillingly; he returned jubilantly. As soon as he came back, he asked his sons to unpack. Now they would never go, he told them. When the Qazi heard this, he was stunned. Fani begged him to leave them alone. It was not for man to defy his destiny, he said. The Qazi kept quiet. I do not know how he reported the matter to Hosh and what his reaction was but thereafter both withdrew and never again brought up the topic.

In the evening, as usual the Palace car came. Fani picked me up and we reached the Hill Fort. There, apart from me, nobody knew that if Fani had not missed the train, he would never have again been in court.

Fani was deeply attached to the court and he had good reason to be so. To have access to the court of the Prince of the Deccan was a matter of great honour. And then to break bread with him and to share his cup! As far as material benefits go, I would say that Fani's luck was not with him in the last phase of his life. On the other hand, misfortune dogged him. Otherwise why should he have declined the offer of the job of a munsif, for which he was well qualified.

That was his first mistake. His other mistakes were his prodigality and improvidence. There were hundreds of employees in the Education Department and the University in the pay scale of Rs 250–400. Every one of them had a family to support. None had to face the troubles that Fani did because they managed to live within their means.

Fani was not able to control his expenditure. Josh had also started in the service in the same scale of pay, and he had stayed in that grade for about two years. He also spent years as a courtier of the Prince and never did he expect or receive financial help from the Prince. Yet he was never in debt.

Honorary courtiership implied that no financial benefit was to be expected from the Prince. In fact, we, who were attached to the Prince, were far better off than the companions and courtiers of the Nizam himself. We dined with the Prince, lolled on comfortable sofas, smoked the costliest cigars and cigarettes, and got sherwanis for Eid. In addition, there were pleasures to satisfy all the senses in abundance at the Prince's court. Every evening was a feast.

In contrast, the Nizam's courtiers had to undergo hard labour indeed. The shifts were so worked that every meal was to be eaten at home. They were never asked to sit in the Nizam's presence and had in fact to stand absolutely still in full court dress, controlling even the smallest desire to scratch or cough.

The following incident illustrates my point. One day I was coming from Kachiguda railway station on my bicycle. Nawab Manzoor Jung's[1] house fell on the way. The Nawab happened to be sitting in the verandah on a cane chair.

We exchanged greetings and since I had not met him for a long time, I went in. There I noticed that one of the servants was wrapping the tape of a cot tightly around his legs. When I enquired about the object of that exercise, he smiled and said he had just come back from the court. 'Because of standing motionless for three hours, my calves have developed cramps. This is the treatment for it.' I began to laugh at this. He joined me and said that the hard labour twice a day had become unbearable. 'But how can one erase what Fate has ordained?'

Manzoor Jung belonged to Delhi or thereabouts. He was a very interesting person and a close friend of the grand old man of Urdu, Moulvi Abdul Haq. At some point, he had served as Collector of some district. His real name was Manzoor Ahmed. He had not yet been titled and so signed the files mostly as 'Manzoor' (This in Urdu also means 'agreed' or 'approved'.) This caused a number of problems in his office. If a petition was presented to him and he signed his name on it and passed it on, the petitioner would start pestering the office maintaining that the petition had been accepted. When such confusion became rampant, the Collector started signing his name in full—Manzoor Ahmed Khan.

Another fatal mistake Fani made was in defaulting in his attendance of the court of Maharaja Kishen Pershad. The Maharaja's decency set him apart and above the nobles of the Deccan, but he was after all human. When he noticed Fani's prolonged neglect and indifference, he cancelled the monthly allowance of Rs 200 that he had hitherto been giving him.

Now Fani had no fixed income. All that he had was the half-pay of his headmastership, which he would get once in six months or so. All of it went to his creditors because all provisions were bought on credit and here those who provided him his necessities on credit must be praised for their patience. His younger son, Feroz Ali Khan, was also a past master at raising credit. Fani still kept on the car. The arrears of the driver's salary kept mounting, as did unpaid petrol bills.

How Fani's plight came to the notice of Alam Ali Khan, an alumnus of Aligarh University, is uncertain. He was then a Judge of the High Court. He had the court of original jurisdiction under him. It was from here that commissions were issued. He started giving those commissions to Fani who thus began to get Rs 300–400 from time to time. Alam Ali Khan was an admirer of Fani. He had had no dealings or association with him. Nor was he on social terms with him. He only helped Fani because both were the alumni of Aligarh. Maybe there was an element of compassion or respect for a man of letters in the act. Be that as it may, with his help Fani could still have saved himself had he sold his car and cut corners. But prudence or providence was no part of Fani's mental makeup. The income from the commissions was of an occasional nature but Fani treated it as a permanent source. It seemed that Fani's flame was on its last flicker. He was like a patient who rallies himself before he finally collapses.

Nawab Shaheed Yar Jung, who was a good poet and a benevolent noble of the Deccan, had considerable influence with the Nizam. He enjoyed the confidence of the Junior Prince. He was genuinely sorry to see Fani in such straitened circumstances. He brought it to the attention of the Prince repeatedly, so much so that finally the Prince agreed to help. He went to his elder brother, the Prince of Berar, who was honorary Commander-in-Chief of the army. The Irregular Forces were also under him. Nawab Qudrat Nawaz Jung, the Princes' maternal uncle, was the commander of this force.

It so happened that there was a vacancy there in the scale of Rs 200–400. The Prince recommended Fani for the post and the Prince of Berar readily agreed.

For an old poet this was a heaven-send—a sinecure for Rs 400 a month. There was no work except to sit on an easy chair, chew paan, and compose poetry. If his misfortune had not made him reject this offer, he would have been having his dinner with the Prince and lunch with Nawab Qudrat Nawaz Jung. Fani would have spent the rest of his life in ease and comfort.

But Fani's genius prompted him to reject the offer. One afternoon as I was checking the accounts of the boarding house, a Hill Fort car pulled up. The driver told me that I had been summoned and that I should get ready in five minutes. Meanwhile he would pick up Fani. I got up nervously. My accountant asked me the reason for such early summons. I replied that perhaps the Prince proposed to go and see a picture. On the way, I told Fani the same thing. But Fani said that it was something else. 'Today His Grace sent me an offer for the Assistant Directorship of the Irregular Forces. Since I have been insolent enough to refuse, I am being called to be reprimanded.' I asked why I had been called if such was the case. Fani replied, 'To set an example. So that you don't commit such insolence ever.' By that time, the car had entered the compound of the Palace. The driver had hardly pulled up in front of the outer steps of the Palace when the Prince emerged in the gallery. We jumped out of the car, made our obeisances, and followed him. The Prince led us to the hall. There was an ornate round table in the centre. The Prince stood on one side of the table while we stood opposite him.

The Prince said, 'Fani, I hear that you have rejected my offer'.

Fani replied with folded hands, 'Sire, the fact of the matter is that a readership in the University in the grade of Rs 350–600 has been fixed for me and the appointment will be made by the end of this month. I stand to lose by the job offered by you since it carries only a scale of Rs 200–400'.

The Prince asked if the appointment had been approved by the University Council.

Fani replied that his belief was founded merely on the promise of a high and responsible official. The insolence of the reply took my breath away but I was powerless to intervene.

The Prince asked for the official's name. Fani replied with considerable pride, 'Nawab Mehdi Yar Jung.'[2]

My heart sank. The Nawab's promises were as liberally bestowed as they were seldom kept. This is not to belittle the Nawab in any way.

His literary tastes were well known. He had been very kind to Josh and me. He lived in great style. He always held two ministerial portfolios simultaneously—some times Political Affairs and Education, some times Finance and Education. He was also the Principal Secretary of the Nizam. At the time of this incident, he was the Minister for Finance and Education. His ability was known all over the state. He was a man of a cheerful disposition and was a successful raconteur. But alongside all this, his forgetfulness was legendry.

One anecdote about his forgetfulness was famous and everyone in the city used to narrate it in his own way. On one Eid day, he went to pray in a public square, taking a young boy with him. He returned home alone forgetting about the existence of the boy completely.

Once I composed a couplet about this trait of his, which he liked very much:

> *Aakilon ka kaul hai, neki kar aur daryaa mien daal*
> *Bhool jaane hi bhi kyaa achchi hai aadat app ki*

> The wise have advised: do good and forget.
> What a noble quality of character you have!

Thus he forgot his promises almost as soon as he made them and anyway would take months to do what he could do in days. In one of my poems, I blamed this on the location of his bungalow, which was the highest on Banjara Hills. Once when he was delaying the fulfilment of one of his promises to me, I provoked him with the following couplet:

> *Aap ke mooras ne waade per diya hai apnaa sar*
> *Aaap ke wade ki zaaman hai shraafat aap ki*

> Your forebear[3] gave his life for his word.
> Your integrity is a security for your word.

The Nawab was beyond himself with joy and praised every word of it. The result was that I got what I wanted. Where have such literary connoisseurs gone?

I have digressed. Let me come back to the story.

The Prince asked Fani if he had anything in writing from the Nawab. Fani still did not get the hint. He replied: 'It is a verbal promise no doubt, Sire, but it is better than a written word.'

The Prince said: 'Alright. If you think you stand to lose by my offer, suit yourself.' The matter ended there. Thereafter the Prince turned to me and we talked on other subjects.

A fortnight elapsed and the moment arrived in anticipation of which Fani had declined the Prince's offer. Full of optimism, Fani went to see the Nawab. He reached at 11.00 a.m. and waited unavailingly with about 35 others. Some people left in disgust by 1.00 p.m. and were wise to do so. At 1.30, an attendant came out and announced that the Nawab Sahib was very busy and would not be able to see anyone that day. Dejected, every one got up and left. Fani alone was to be spared five minutes of the Nawab's time. The attendant warned him to be brief. Fani went in and salaamed. The Nawab did not return his greetings but simply motioned him to a seat. As soon as he sat down, the attendant came and announced that lunch was ready. The Nawab asked him: 'Mr Fani, of Atish and Nasikh, whom do you consider the better poet? Give good reasons for your preference.'

This was a typical tactic employed by Nawab Mehdi Yar Jung with those whom he wanted to put off. Josh will enjoy this very much because he himself has had to answer this question many times. The Nawab would follow this question up with another: 'Well, what do you think of Tabatabai's poetry?'

Here I must digress once more since I was witness to just such an exchange myself. Once Josh and I went to see the Nawab for a favour. The Nawab wanted to avoid the subject, and noticing that Josh was trying to raise it, he asked him: 'Mr Josh, whom do you consider a better poet, Atish or Nasikh?' Josh, in order to get his work done, repeated the opinion he had delivered scores of times before. The Nawab listened with such rapt attention and apparent relish as if he was hearing it for the first time. As soon as Josh finished, the Nawab shot off his second question: 'Well, what do you think about the poetry of Tabatabai? Josh was stung by this blatant evasiveness. His hot Pathan blood boiled in anger and, forgetting that he had gone there for a favour, he shot back: 'What has that joker to do with poetry? There are thousands of things he could do—mend shoes, make crackers, sharpen knives, polish utensils. Where was the need for him to write poetry?'

The Nawab could not stomach such outright denunciation of his favourite poet. He got up and said brusquely: 'Well, Mr Josh, we will meet some other time. Right now I am very busy.' We salaamed and came out. The purpose of the visit was defeated. This was what the Nawab had intended. I told Josh that his outburst had lost him the chance to get his work done.

Josh asked me why I thought so. I said because the Minister had great regard for Tabatabai. Josh fulminated: 'Such regard be damned. Why did he provoke me? You tell me how would you have responded to such a meaningless question?' I replied, 'I would have said he was a very learned man—without a peer in this land. He was unique.' Josh was upset. He said, 'The question was about his poetry.' I said, 'The Nawab is a shrewd person. He would have understood that I admire his learning, not his poetry.' Josh retorted in anger, 'To hell with it. My work will not be done. But now he will never ask me this question again.'

To get back to Fani's interview with the Nawab, after Fani had finished comparing Atish and Nasikh as he had been asked to, he suddenly remembered the attendant's warning that whatever he wanted to say, he should say quickly. So he brought himself to submit that the day after there was a meeting of the University Council in which the decision on the filling up of the vacancy was to be taken. 'I had come here to remind Your Honour about that.' The Minister replied casually, 'Mr Fani, I have found a better person for that job. I'll consider your case later.'

The splendid castle, that Fani had been building in the air for a month came crashing down. Now Fani was ruing his rejection of the offer made by the Prince. But that vacancy had also been filled up in the meantime. He had lost the bird in hand in unsuccessful pursuit of the two in the bush.

He was finally forced to consider disposing of the car. But he did not mention this to anyone. One day he drove quietly to an auction house and left the car there for disposal. When the auctioneer asked how much he expected for it, he said not a whit less than Rs 800.

Fani's car was in such good condition that it would have been considered a good buy for Rs 800. But his ill luck dogged him there too. Nobody made a bid for more than Rs 300. So the auction was postponed. However, the auctioneer claimed his commission of two annas in a rupee (12½ per cent). Fani was so disgusted that he told the auctioneer to dispose of the car at the next auction at whatever price he could get. It was sold for Rs 300 at the next auction. After the deduction of the commission of the two auctions, what Fani got in hand was hardly enough to meet the arrears of the pay of the driver's salary.

It was then that Fani told me about his latest misfortune. But after the car had been disposed of, there was nothing one could do for Fani. Those who do not believe in fate should draw a lesson from Fani's story. How well has Saadi, the Persian poet, put it:

> Even if one has two hundred skills
> They won't avail, if one is unlucky.

The Curse of Alcohol

EID WAS OVER but many of the nautch girls stayed on for a while. Nine taxis had been hired on the Prince's account, to be at their disposal twenty-four hours a day. Each taxi charged Rs 20 per day. After breakfast, they would sally forth in a grand procession of cars led by one in which Shyam sat tightly ensconced with one of the beauties. They presented a spectacle that caused people to stare in wonder wherever they passed by with their exotic passengers. Struck by the scene, I composed a poem.

These women would amuse themselves thus till 1.00 in the afternoon. Then, in the evening, they would get ready for gatherings later at the Prince's court.

There they would sit at their appointed places. For some time, Dhimmak Jung kept up an offended silence against the plump matron seated by his side. But he eventually thawed and began to chat with her. During the seven days the ladies continued as the Prince's guests, they got much more from their generous host than they would usually have earned in a year. The pockets of agents also jingled with silver and gold coins.

Shyam did not get anything at all out of his exertions except all sorts of blame. 'That dancer didn't get breakfast on time; there was no proper lighting in so and so's lodge; the one from Lucknow had to wait long for her lunch;

the other one from Agra got her paans too late, and so on.' Shyam accepted the blame by cursing himself and slapping his face and this added to the fun of the complainants.

In the midst of all this tumult and bustle, one day Fani said to me, 'You have become close to the Prince very quickly. But remember one thing. You will not long be able to remain a teetotaller. Soon I shall see you ranged amongst the tipplers.' I replied that God had kept me safe for three years. I could not say what would happen next. Hardly had a month elapsed since Fani's warning when one evening a car pulled up in front of my door. I asked about Fani. The driver said that he had only been ordered to fetch me. I dressed and got into the car. The car pulled up outside a strange house instead of going to the Hill Fort. It looked like the house of a noble. As I stepped inside, a handsome servant came and motioned me to follow him. After crossing many well-appointed rooms, we reached a small courtyard. There, neatly arranged on a beautiful carpet were four easy chairs. Seated on the chair in the centre was the Prince. On his left sat a young woman of striking beauty. I made my courtly salaams to the Prince and stood there respectfully. The Prince said to me graciously, 'Sidq, you know our agent in Bombay. He has sent me this rare gift. Knowing your discriminating taste for beauty, I have called you first of all and I am keen to know your opinion about her.' I folded my hands and said in a couplet:

Khudaa aabaad rakhe hum safeeraan-e-gulistaan ko
Jo koi phool khiltaa hai to hum ko yaad karte hain

God bless my garden-mates, may they live long!
Whenever a bud blossoms, they think of me.

The Prince was so delighted to hear this that his face lit up. He addressed the young woman: 'He is Sidq Jaisi, our court poet. See what an appropriate couplet he has recited.' She regarded me with kindly eyes and raised her delicate hand in salutation. In return, I placed both my hands on my heart and bowed my head. Then the Prince started praising my intelligence, my wit, and my poetry. I wish he had only asked me to sit down. He probably forgot to do so and I could not take a seat on my own. That was against court etiquette. At every word of praise, I had to do seven floor salaams. It wore me out. But there was no escape. After perhaps an hour, the woman took pity on me and asked the Prince innocently why I did not sit. The Prince, as if startled by this question, asked me, 'Why don't you sit down?'

I made seven salaams in response to this question, which implied an invitation, and collapsed into a chair.

The Prince then introduced her to me. 'She is called Najma'. I said, 'Sarkar, I am afraid of Mr Najm, otherwise I would have said it is a lovely name.' The Prince laughed at this. Meanwhile I had a good look at her. I was wondering what part of her to praise, on which to compose a couplet, and on which to write a complete poem. I contented myself by reciting a Persian couplet in my own heart for the time.

The Prince started describing his visit to Bombay and the abundance of beauty there. I listened attentively and interjected from time to time only to express agreement. At 9 p.m. the ADCs arrived. Two or three nobles and a few paid courtiers followed them. Last in was our friend Kammo. There were only about a dozen courtiers that day. Fani, Piya, Carew, Ummak Jung, Dhimmak Jung were all absent. I discreetly asked an ADC the reason for their absence. He replied, 'This is a special circle. They belong to the general group. They can't come to this gathering.'

At 10.00, a servant placed a teapoy in front of the Prince, another in front of the guest of the evening—and then in front of the other guests. Another servant placed two bottles of a fire-coloured liquid in front of the Prince. On another teapoy, he placed a dish containing minced meat of lamb's liver and kidney. The room was filled with the aroma of the dish. At a signal, a servant opened the cork of a bottle which looked different from others. The Prince himself poured out the drinks, and while he did so, I was reminded of a couplet of the Nizam's poetic preceptor, Jaleel:

> *Saaqi! Teri sharaab jo sheeshe mein thi pari*
> *Saagar mein aa ke aur bhi saanche mein dhal gai!*

> O cupbearer! Wine, a fairy in thy bottle
> Acquired contours when poured into a peg!

The Prince put one peg in front of himself. He offered one to his beautiful guests. Then he signalled to her to offer me one. The contents of the other bottle were then served to the others. Whoever was offered a peg, would get up, do seven salaams to the Prince, and then take the peg. The lady got up with the peg in her hand and came to offer it to me. I got up nervously and submitted to the Prince with folded hands, 'Sarkar, please spare me. Far from drinking it, I had till today never ever seen how alcohol looks.' But it seemed that the Prince was determined to make me drink that day. He remarked, 'What a pity! You do not see who is deigning to serve you. Only the lucky get such an opportunity. You will remember for the rest of your life that you had your first drink from the hands of such a beauty.'

I kept on declining humbly but the Prince would not listen. He said somewhat impatiently, 'If you do not accept her offer, I shall no longer remain a votary of your poetry. A composer of love poetry rejecting an offer from such a belle! How can I believe that you are a poet?' At last, he said that if I would not accept the peg from her, he himself would have to get up to offer it to me. I realized then there was no escape. I accepted the drink, got up, and salaamed the Prince again. This pleased him. He said that was a sensible thing to do. I took God's name and took a sip. It tasted as bitter as neem water. I couldn't help making a face.

The Prince smiled and said, 'I gave you a very light drink. It is called champagne and is known as a ladies' drink. 'Then, pointing towards the other courtiers, he said, 'They are having the real stuff—brandy. It is very strong. Since you are not used to drinking, I started with champagne.' I began to copy the others and sipped slowly.

I was suddenly reminded of something that had happened when I was young. Qazi Mir Muhammad[1] had drawn up my horoscope, in which amongst other predictions, he had said that one day I would consume alcohol. At that time, I had objected to this but the Qazi had observed that he was only stating what was there in my stars. Now his prophecy was being fulfilled in this way!

After some time I felt inebriated and doubtless, cheerful and light. At long last, it struck midnight and the drinks were removed. By this time Kammo had consumed ten pegs of brandy. His eyes were red and his voice slurred but he answered the Prince with folded hands. He still knew where he was sitting. The others too had taken five or six pegs each but nobody was tipsy. All of them still meticulously observed etiquette. I concluded that misbehaviour after drinking was largely a matter of show and pretension.

At a signal from the Prince, Moiz and Bindu started readying their instruments and the official mushaira started. Used to eating early, I was famished. The Prince addressed me: 'Sidq, today you are alone [without Fani]. You will have to certify the quality of each couplet by making a suitable response'. He didn't know that I was writhing with hunger? But there was no way out. It was my bad luck that Fani was not there; otherwise we would have divided the job of making seemingly spontaneous responses to the Prince's poetry between ourselves. But in his absence, I had to bear the burden all by myself.

The mushaira ended finally at 2 a.m. The Prince said to the ADC, 'Today Sidq has suffered a great deal. See whether the dinner is ready.' On being told that it was ready, the Prince got up. He asked me to go and have a wash. I complied and reached the dining room within minutes. Everybody else was already there.

On the Prince's right sat Najma. I was asked to sit to his left. I salaamed and took my seat. It was nearly 3.00 in the morning and it felt as if we were going to eat *sehari* (a meal that Muslims take before daybreak during Ramadan, the month of fasting. For the rest of the day, till sunset, they cannot eat or drink anything). By now I had lost my appetite. At the dining table the Prince remarked, 'Because of our dear guest, you must be noticing some element of formality at dinner. The delay has occurred because of that. But I could not have asked her to share our simple daily fare. Every religion enjoins hospitality for the guest.' I added, 'Particularly if the guest is beautiful.' The Prince liked my comment and repeated it. Then he asked for an example. I recited a couplet:

> *Mehmaan-e-haseen kaabil-e-izzat hai jidhar jaae*
> *Aankhon mein thehar jaae keh seene me utar jaae*

> A comely guest commands respect wherever she goes,
> She has a choice: stay in my eyes, or abide in the heart.

The Prince said that the second hemistich had added to the value of the couplet. 'How lovely!' he remarked, 'Encore; Encore.' Obediently, I repeated it. Then the Prince said, 'Like me you must have also hardly noticed the passage of time because of her. It is nearly dawn but I feel as if I've just come.' On that, I recited a couplet with folded hands:

> *Zulfon peh kabhi phool se chehre par nazar jaai*
> *Kyaa waqt hai woh bhi jo huzoori main guzar jaai*

> Gazing at your tresses or ogling the flower face.
> Ah! The time spent in your attendance!

The Prince exclaimed: 'Very beautiful', and added: 'The use of the term '*huzoori*' (attendance) cannot be praised enough. As far as my knowledge goes, no poet has made such brilliant use of it as you have done.' Najma added with an enchanting smile: 'He composes very well, indeed.' On that, the Prince remarked to me: 'This is a high point in your poetry. Her simple praise must afford you more satisfaction than if Maharaja Kishen Pershad or Sir Akbar[2] or some other big gun had praised your poetry.' I got up and salaamed first the Prince and then Najma. She acknowledged my salutation with captivating coquetry. After dinner, I was permitted to go home.

Next day I wrote to Qazi Mir Muhammad congratulating him on the accuracy of his prediction. I told him how I had had, under compulsion, to drink alcohol the previous night. The Qazi was very happy. He took it as certification of his knowledge of astrology.

The Prince never asked me to join him in drinking at common gatherings. On special occasions, I joined him but they were no more than three or four in a year.

The next day I told Fani about what had happened the previous night. He too seemed pleased that his forecast had proved true. He said, 'It is good that you did not decline the Princes offer. I think he will not force you in future. His object in making you drink was that there should be no "dry" person in that colourful party.' When I related how I had to stand for three hours and to suffer without food till 2 a.m., he said with a hearty laugh, 'That is nothing. I have undergone a much greater ordeal. Thank God, you were not in the court then. Otherwise, you would have packed up the next day.'

It was during the rainy season. The sky was overcast that evening with lightning and thunder threatening. The Prince suddenly ordered his ADC to arrange dinner in the lawn. Then he looked towards the lawn and said, 'The weather is good. We will enjoy eating outside.' Piya folded his hands, got up, and seconded the Prince's suggestion, saying, 'Yes, Sarkar. God be praised. Your Lordship is just like your grandfather. Our late blessed Sarkar also used to eat on the lawn during the rainy season.' He recited a couplet to reinforce what he had said. The Prince was glad to find such support of his view. After two minutes, the Prince got up followed by about 40–45 courtiers. I looked at the sky and trembled with trepidation. It was so dark that one could not see one's own hand. Only the Prince's passage was lit like the day. The electrical engineer had already reached the lawn and started his work. Every tree had bulbs of different colours hung from its branches. The entire lawn was bathed in many splendoured lights. As the Prince took his seat, the first course was served. It was as if the rain was waiting for the signal. The clouds burst and it began to pour filling up the soup with water. The Prince put down his spoon and addressed Piya. 'Piya, the soup is delicious today.' Piya responded with folded hands, 'Well said, Sir. I too am enjoying it more than on other days.' The rain came down in torrents as soon as the plates were removed. That evening, the Princess (Niloufer) also happened to be present at dinner. The Prince suggested that she should have her dinner sent for in her chambers. She got up at once and went inside. I expected that we too would get up and move but although the rain was becoming progressively heavier, the dinner continued to be served unabated. By the time two courses had been served, all of us were thoroughly drenched. Dhimmak Jung showed his worth that day. He sat collected throughout with such dignity as if he were posing for a photograph. The dishes as they were served up were so watery that they were completely bland and unfit for consumption. I couldn't manage more than a morsel of any dish. Luckily with the number of courses, even a morsel of each went some way towards appeasing my hunger.

The Prince sat at the head of the table with complete unconcern. All the time the velocity of the downpour kept on increasing. At the end of dinner, the Prince washed his hand with great composure. After that, he had his paan and started picking his teeth with the same equanimity. Then the servants started washing the hands of the courtiers though that day washing the hands was a joke.

The Prince started talking to Piya about the pilgrimage of Raba Basri. I thought I was in a nightmare. In a short while, I would open my eyes and find myself in my warm cozy bed. But water was getting into my eyes and dream itself was an illusion. After fifteen minutes, the Prince got up from his chair. We followed suit. The Prince began to walk leisurly as if he were strolling in the garden on a normal day. Suddenly, he turned around and addressed Piya, 'Raba Basri was really a great lady of her time.' Piya folded his hands and said, 'Right, Sire, we have heard from our elders that all the great spiritual leaders of her time used to pay their respects to her.' In this manner, with the Prince conversing casually, stopping off and on, we entered the gallery of Hill Fort. There, under shelter at last, we felt a little warm.

Leaving us there in that state, the Prince went into his bathroom and emerged after about five minutes in fresh clothes. I was hoping that we too would be allowed to go home and rest, or at least that the Comptroller would be asked to give us a change of dress. But instead, the Prince went and sat on his chair in the Darbar Hall. We were all called in one by one. Moiz and Bindu sat on the platform and the mushaira began.

I told Fani that since he was not given to lying or exaggerating, I was bound to accept the story as true. Fani replied that it was as true as it was 5 p.m. then. 'And believe me those wet clothes dried on our bodies by 3 a.m. Only then were we allowed to go home. Now tell me: was your ordeal greater than this?' I admitted that his hardship had been the greater. I added that I was sorry I had not been present at that dinner. Otherwise, when the Prince made for the Palace, I would have suggested to him humbly that since the weather was fine, why not have the mushaira also on the lawn? Fani broke into a guffaw.

Jhumman's Insolence

IT WAS LATE AFTERNOON by the time I returned home after hearing Fani's amazing story. That day, I ate something at home before going to the Prince so that I could survive the ordeal. By the time I finished, it was 8 p.m. The car came to fetch me without Fani. I proceeded alone to the house of the previous evening on Red Hills. The same handsome servant greeted me and asked me to follow him. After passing through a number of rooms and galleries, he stopped in front of a new room and asked me to wait there while he went inside and announced me. I was called in immediately.

That day the Prince was sitting in a hall of mirrors. By his side was Najma. The carpet, furnishings, and hangings in this room were very rich. The walls were painted pink. The ceiling had beautiful engravings. There were numerous mirrors, none less than 7 feet in height.

As soon as I was face to face with the Prince, I made my courtly bows, which he acknowledged with a faint smile. Then, placing both my hands on my heart I bowed my head to the beauty. The Prince asked me to sit down.

I salaamed again and was about to sit in the chair in front of him when he said, 'No, not there. Sit by our side'. I did seven salaams again, and with folded hands submitted, 'How can a slave sit by the side of the master?' The Prince replied, 'We are ordering you to.' I again salaamed seven times and took my seat next to the Prince. Meanwhile Shyam was announced and summoned. It was apparent, he had taken great pains with his appearance—well-trimmed beard, moustaches dyed in a Japanese dye, new sherwani, new headdress, a borrowed waist belt, cheap unpolished pumps on his feet, and a dozen odd stains of paan spit on the pajama. He made his salaams and was asked to sit by the lady's side. Shyam took his seat casually—no salaams, no thanks, as if it were an informal gathering. The Prince asked him, '*Baghlol* [fool, silly, or stupid]. Did you arrange for her lunch properly? There was no dearth of anything?' Shyam replied with folded hands, 'With the grace of my Lord, there was no dearth of anything. This slave of yours had taken enough food for ten people. And she was all by herself—except of course for me!'

The Prince smiled, turned to me, and said, 'Sidq, we have given the title of Baghlol to Shyam. What is your opinion?' I got up and said with folded hands, 'Very appropriate indeed.' Najma burst into laughter at that. Shyam looked daggers at me.

The Prince then said, 'You see his splendour all around today. It is not necessary to look at him; look anywhere, you will see him [because of the mirrors].' I recited a couplet:

Jade hain har taraf khilwat-khade mein un ke aaine
Tan tanhaa chala karti hain choten her muqaabal se

Her private chambers are studded with glass
Alone, she battles with her rivals surrounding her.

The Prince liked the couplet very much. Najma also enjoyed it.

After some time Carew arrived. The Prince welcomed him heartily. 'Come, Carew. Yesterday in a hurry I forgot to invite you. You bring life to a party.' Carew thanked him profusely and sat down by my side. He was followed by the other guests of the previous night.

That day a dancing girl from Lucknow had been called for the entertainment of the honoured guest. After some time, we heard the sound of the musical instruments from the courtyard. The Prince got up and proceeded there. The show started. At one point, the hem of the dancer's sari kissed Carew's white beard. He frowned. The Prince started laughing and told me, 'Sidq, he is my teacher. I respect him greatly. For that reason whenever a beauty comes to my parties, I get the hem of her sari touched by his beard by way of benediction so that her sins are washed away.' Carew remarked crossly: 'Very well said, Sire.' Everyone, including the beauty, laughed at his annoyance. Time flew by in such merrymaking and flippancy. Soon dinner was ordered.

At dinner Najma was seated to the right of the Prince. I was asked to sit to his left. Next to me were the ADC and the rest of the courtiers. On Najma's right sat Shyam and then others. Poor Fani, Ummak Jung, and Dhimmak Jung and other general courtiers were missing that day too.

The table was laden with delicacies. The biryani was particularly delicious. But my eyes were fixed on Najma's face. More than the food, I was relishing her beauty. I was musing on the power of wealth that was able to attract such a beauty from Bombay to Hyderabad. How lucky the Prince was whose court was graced by such beauty! After dinner, the Prince made

Princess Niloufer (wife of Prince Muazzam Jah),
niece of the last Caliph of Turkey Abdul Majeed.

Prince Muazzam Jah

The Hill Fort Palace in 1999, now unused.

Maharaja Kishen Pershad
(Prime Minister 1900–12; 1926–36)

some small talk. Piya also was not invited to such gatherings. Only young people were called. The Prince addressed only me and so I was literally on tenterhooks. A small lapse and I would be finished. The Prince told me that in the morning someone had come from Lucknow with a letter of recommendation from the Raja of Mehmoodabad. He had been put up at the Nizamia Hotel. 'You will meet him at the Hill Fort. He also composes poetry.' I asked for his pen-name. The Prince did not remember but said it was something that rhymed with *bhains* (buffalo). At this Najma broke into laughter. I said, 'Maybe he does sport the pen-name of bhains. After all it is unique.' The Prince also laughed but said it was not that but something which rhymed with it.

Suddenly the Prince looked at his watch. 'It is 2.30. Time for you to go. But before you go, narrate a joke which should make our guest laugh.'

I folded my hands and said, 'Last July there was a mushaira at the Warangal College. Since your Lordship was at Ooty [a famous hill station in Tamil Nadu], I was free. My friends from Warangal had also been pressing me to go there. So I went. The hall was packed to capacity on the night of the mushaira. A few students of the college recited their poems. Then a teacher, Muhammad Ismail Zabeeh, got up. Every one looked at him expectantly. He started:

> *Nikalne ko to hasrat wasl ki ai naazeen nikli*
> *Magar jaisi niklani chaahiye waisi nahin nikli*

> My yearning for union did find a vent
> But not, o' love, to my heart's content.

From a corner of the hall, someone shouted: 'In this regard, Sir, we feel you, not she were to blame.' The hall broke into peels of laughter at this remark. The Principal also rolled with laughter. Pandemonium broke lose. The poet could not proceed further. He tore his paper and mouthing abuse, left the hall.

The Prince was in splits. So was Najma. The Prince laughed so much that tears welled up in his eyes. The servants rushed to him with napkins. It was 3 a.m. The Prince allowed me to go home.

The festivities lasted a fortnight. Like all good things, they came to an end. Our dear guest also departed. That evening when the car came to pick me up, Fani was sitting in it. He smiled and said, 'These last two weeks you have enjoyed yourself to the full. Now again it is Hill Fort and us—the same old faces and the same old story.'

At dinner, I saw a new face. It occurred to me that he must be the man whom the Prince had mentioned in the house at Red Hills. Presently the Prince introduced him.

Sidq, the gentleman sitting opposite you is the one who brought a letter from the Raja of Mehmoodabad. His name is Jhumman. He sports the nom-de-plume of Taish [meaning anger]. He is a partner in some circus. Raja Sahib has requested me to help him get a suitable location for the circus. I have issued instructions to the Kotwal accordingly. The field opposite the Putli Bowli would probably be a fit place for the purpose.

Fani responded with folded hands. 'The best thing is that the place is in the centre of the city.' Ummak Jung put in: 'All the good circuses which have so far come here used the same ground.' Dhimmak Jung added, 'Sarkar has proposed a very good site. It is difficult to find a better place in the city.' The Prince remarked that he had great regard for Raja Sahib.

Dinner ended. When the almond-and-cream pudding was served, the Prince himself put a large helping of cream in a plate, added two almonds and two pistachios and, offering the plate to Jhumman, said, 'Jhumman you belong to Lucknow. It is famous for its cream. Just taste our cream also.' That crude fellow accepted the plate without saying any thanks, took a spoonful, shook his head, and simply said, '*Hoon*. Not bad!'

The Prince looked at Fani and me and smiled. We also smiled. I was surprised that the Raja of Mehmoodabad, whose lowliest servants were so well mannered, had sent to this court such an unpolished rustic. I could not believe that he belonged to Lucknow or was even remotely connected to the court of the Raja. But the Prince himself had said that the man had come with a recommendation from the Raja.

After dinner, out of courtesy, the Prince asked him to recite his poem. He bored us with two or three ghazals. The Prince regretted his impulse. He told Jhumman to rest and assured him that he would call him later. After Jhumman had left, the Prince asked Piya, 'You heard him?' Piya said, 'It was utter trash.' The Prince added, 'What I mean is that the compositions of Fani and Sidq relate to the heart. But this man's poetry had nothing to do with the heart.' Ummak Jung and Dhimmak Jung added in chorus. 'Goodness gracious! He is only a poetaster. He has nothing to do with poetry.'

The Prince repeated, 'I say that his poetry has nothing to do with the heart'. I got up with folded hands and said, 'Sir, it has nothing to do even with the head.' Fani guffawed heartily at this. Others joined him. The Prince also laughed loudly. Then he said, 'According to me his poetry is not connected with the heart. According to you, it is not connected with the head. Then with which organ is it connected?' I submitted, 'This is not the proper place to mention that. But everyone here is a man of intelligence. They will catch the hint.'

The Prince turned to Piya: 'See Sidq's intelligence!' Piya laughed and said, 'My Lord only such sharp minds can survive in the company of kings and princes.' I got up and salaamed Piya gratefully for his kind words.

Piya proceeded,

You may not have heard the story of Nadir Shah and Mirza Mehdi. When Nadir Shah reached the banks of the Attock River in the first phase of his invasion of India, Mirza Mehdi, his secretary, was with him. The invader asked his secretary, 'Mirza, can you tell me which food is only one morsel in size but is more delicious than any other in the world?'

Mirza Mehdi replied respectfully: 'Hen's egg, Your Majesty.'

After that Nadir Shah got busy with his military campaigns and the conversation did not proceed further. Years later, after the sack of Delhi, when returning home, Nadir Shah stopped at the bank of the Attock and suddenly remembered the inconclusive conversation. He asked Mehdi, 'With what?'

'With salt and pepper, Your Majesty', replied Mehdi coolly. The ruler was pleased and the courtiers were impressed with Mirza's brilliance.

All the courtiers enjoyed this anecdote very much. Suddenly the Prince asked me, 'Sidq, recite a couplet which has nothing to do with heart but is connected with the head.' I complied:

> *Saatveen shab apne kothe par woh maah paraa chadhaa*
> *Dono tukde mil gaye, ik chaand poora ho gayaa.*

> Evening of half-moon, she stood on the terrace
> The two halves met; the moon became full.

The Prince and Fani together jumped up. All the courtiers were also vociferous in their applause. The Prince said to Fani: 'What a couplet Sidq has recited!' Fani said that he was not surprised. 'Sidq remembers tomes of poetry by rote.'

The Prince then turned towards me. 'Can you recite for me a couplet which, though meaningful, is beyond my comprehension. Only, it should not have any archaic or difficult word.' Fani interrupted, 'I too should not be able to understand it.' I said, God willing, I shall recite such a couplet:

Tasveer-e-kohna par bhi rahin bad-gumaaniyaan
Khat unke jis ke paas gaye be-ticket gaye

Suspicion didn't spare even old pictures,
She always sent letters without stamps.

The Prince, Fani, and all the courtiers were at a loss about the meaning of this couplet. I leave the court in this condition for some time so that my readers too may rack their brains to decipher the meaning of this couplet.

The Horsemanship of Dagh

UMMAK JUNG AND DHIMMAK JUNG too tried their best to deconstruct the couplet but without luck.

At last, the Prince asked Fani if he understood the meaning. Fani replied in the negative. The Prince then asked me the author's name. I said it was written by Munir Shikohabadi. Fani said Munir was a master and could not have written meaningless verse. Ummak Jung and Dhimmak Jung said they had not even heard his name. I said he was attached to the court of the Nawab of Rampur. Once Nawab Yusuf Ali Khan heard his ghazal, which ended:

Sharmindaa khud hoon apne kamaalon ke saamne

I blush at the enormity of my own talents.

The Nawab then wrote a couplet saying, 'Why should you blush when people like me are your admirers?' and invited Munir to join his court. Munir spent the rest of his life there.

The Prince said: 'See how the princes in the past honoured men of excellence!' Piya commented: 'No doubt, but nowhere were such people more honoured than in Hyderabad. The late sixth Nizam paid Dagh[1] in one go at the rate of Rs 1000 per month for ten years when he employed him. The amount was delivered in bullock-carts laden with coins at the residence of Dagh.'

The Prince asked 'Why? Had he not been paid for ten years?'

Piya replied,

'No, Sire, Dagh was not even employed earlier. The fact is that after the death of Nawab Kalb Ali Khan of Rampur there was no one who could appreciate the great talent of Dagh. Men of merit lost their patronage in Rampur. Dagh came to Hyderabad. But to gain access to the Nizam wasn't easy. Dagh stayed in a small house in the city and used to visit the nobles of the State. He spent ten years like that without being able to gain access to the Nizam. His renown, however, spread all over the State. In the city one special mushaira used to be held every month and in that Dagh would cast a spell on the audience with his recitation. Your humble slave has not seen a poet with a better voice or greater command over the language. After the mushaira, everyone amongst the audience could be heard reciting two or three of his couplets. When his fame spread in the city, I took permission of his late Highness and attended one of those mushairas. The gathering was at the residence of the two brothers Sama Jung and Samak Jung [sic]. Dagh's turn came at 2 a.m. His opening couplet created a furore. I still remember it:

> Allah re tallawun, abhi kyaa the, abhi kyaa ho
> Shokhi ho to shokhi ho, hayaa ho to hayaa ho.

God! how capricious and mercurial is your temperament
Now coquettish, now coy—you've mastered all moods.

The audience leapt up from their seats and kept on shouting 'encore' and Dagh, swayed by his own rhythm, obliged. His seventh or eighth couplet was this:

> Is dil se mujhe laag hai, be-maher to main hoon.
> Tum shaane wafaa, kaane wafaa, jaane wafaa ho.

I am inclined towards that heart, heartless though I be
Mine of love, pride of love, you're the life of love indeed.

Virtual pandemonium broke out at this couplet. I too was beyond myself. I wanted to rush and embrace Dagh.

The Prince cut in, 'I hope you weren't guilty of such an unbecoming act.'

Piya replied, 'No, Sire. How could I get the opportunity in such a gathering?' Then, he continued,

In short, when the whole city was resounding to the praise of Dagh, Maharaja Kishen Pershad one day talked of him to the late Nizam. The Nizam sent for him, heard him, and was swept off his feet. He was effusive in his praise. From then on Dagh was sent for to join the Nizam at dinner. He would stand for hours in front of the Nizam. But he did not get any job, or even a gift. But we knew that his star would soon shine on the firmament of the Deccan.

A year passed like that and none of us had the courage to bring Dagh's plight to the notice of His Highness.

Then, one day, the late Nizam went on a hunt. In the jungle, all of a sudden, he thought of Dagh. He asked Maharaja Bahadur to have Dagh fetched immediately. Within two hours, Dagh was presented before the Nizam.

On the evening of the second day, the late Nizam was sitting on a chair in an open field. All the courtiers and members of the staff were standing respectfully on either side.

Some riders were giving a demonstration of their horsemanship. The Nizam was watching each of them with great interest. One refractory horse was giving a lot of trouble to his rider but the latter was an expert. He sat on the back of the horse like a nail riveted to a piece of wood.

All of a sudden the Nizam turned to Dagh and asked him: 'Dagh, have you ever done any riding?' He replied with folded hands that in his youth he had done so but years had gone by since then. The Nizam said: 'Alright, show me your riding skills today.' Dagh had no choice but to comply. At a signal from the Nizam, the stubborn horse was brought to Dagh. Poor Dagh got on to the horse nervously. As soon as he did so, the horse trainer cracked his whip on the beast. In an instant Dagh was somersaulting on the ground and the horse had bolted away towards the jungle.

Dagh was picked up. Fortunately, he was not hurt. He dusted himself, came, and stood before the Nizam who was rolling with laughter. When he recovered, he addressed Dagh: 'You are a good rider. I appoint you as my head syce.' Dagh made his grateful bows. The Nizam then asked him, 'How long have you been in our State?'

'Ten years, Sire.'

The Nizam turned to his Prime Minister and said: 'We appoint Dagh as the court poet on a salary of Rs 1000 per month. His salary with arrears for the last ten years should be paid right away.' The Maharaja folded his hands, said, 'Yes Sire,' and went to attend to the matter at once. A dispatch rider was rushed with orders to the treasurer in the city for compliance. The Nizam then retired to his tent and all the nobles in attendance swarmed around Dagh to congratulate him.

The next day the whole city saw carts loaded with silver carrying Dagh's ten years' arrears of salary arrive with police escort at Dagh's house. The house on Abid Road where advocate Khem Chand now lives was the house in which Dagh was staying at that time. The appearance of the house has changed now but the money came to that very house and Dagh stayed in that house for the rest of his life.

A spell was cast on the court by the narration of this story of extraordinary and whimsical magnanimity.

After a while, the Prince asked me: 'Do you yourself know the meaning of this couplet?' I submitted that I would try to explain the meaning of the couplet according to my limited understanding. 'It is up to Your Grace to accept or reject the explanation.'

'Go ahead,' commanded the Prince.

I said that the poet lived during the reign of Queen Victoria. The Empress of India was known for her beauty. Her likeness was printed on postal stamps, which were affixed on all envelopes.

'The poet's beloved is so full of mistrust and jealousy that whenever she replies to the letters of her lover, she doesn't stick any stamp on the cover lest the lover should be carried away by the beauty of the Queen and ignore her. So, she sends her letters without any stamps.'

The Prince said. 'That still leaves the "oldness" of the picture unexplained. Why did the poet call the picture "old"?'

I replied: 'The stamps are not printed everyday. They are printed in millions. A stamp printed in 1890 would still be in use in 1900. Hence, the reference to the "oldness" of the picture.'

The Prince laughed and said, 'Is it a couplet or a riddle? One has to decipher rather then understand it.' Fani said it required both understanding of poetry and a capacity to solve riddles. 'I wouldn't ever have thought of the Queen Empress and my mind would have remained entangled in this puzzle for months.'

The Prince remarked to Fani, 'Note Sidq's spontaneity and quick-wittedness. It is if he was ready to recite this couplet.'

Fani said, 'Didn't I tell you, Sire, that he remembers volume upon volume of poetry by heart?'

Now, at a signal from the Prince, both Moiz and Bindu took their seats on the dais and started playing their instruments. The 'official' mushaira thus started. On the first hemistich, Najm Afandi raised his right hand in mid air, exhibiting extreme absorption on his face. At the second line, he waved his hand in the air as if defending himself from an imaginary stone thrown at him. That was how he exhibited his effusive praise of the Prince's ghazals.

Najm is one of my sincere friends and my apologies to him but I shall be faithful to the details. The same holds good for Mahirul Qadri also. When I have not hidden anything about myself, why should I spare others?

I shall also ask for forgiveness of the Prince and his distinguished elder brother. If I take any liberty with facts, I shall be responsible before them and my God. My purpose is to draw a faithful portrait so that those who have not seen the court can at least picture it.

Najm, because of his naïveté and inexperience and his proximity to the Prince, had come to believe that there could not be any change in his position. He would treat the Prince as a teacher would an ordinary pupil even in front of others. He did not realize that the courtly world was different from the ordinary world.

The teachers and tutors of Princes and rulers have to behave towards their wards just like other ordinary servants do.

One day at the court of Maharaja Sir Kishen Pershad, the Prime Minister of the State, about fifty people were sitting with him, including Josh and me. One of his granddaughters, hardly four years old, came rushing in. Old courtiers in their sixties stood up respectfully and did their seven salaams to her with the same show of reverence as for the Maharaja.

I could not understand who was being salaamed. But I also did what everybody else was doing. After I sat down, I noticed that a little girl was sitting in the lap of the Maharaja. It then dawned on me that all this show of respect was for that chit of a girl.

When we came out of the Maharaja's court, Josh was bitter. He said, 'See where our misfortune has brought us! We have to get up to honour an infant girl, who doesn't even understand what all the fuss is about!' I consoled him, advocating patience. 'After ten years when the child grows into youth, the smile with which she will return your salutation will be your reward.' '*Insha Allah, Insha Allah*,' muttered Josh as he got into his car. Then he added, 'We will have to wait patiently for that day.' I remarked that the fruits of patience were always sweet. 'Indeed, Indeed,' said Josh and forgot his anger in contemplation of the future. He did not mention this incident again to anyone, though he had a habit of repeating and recounting incidents which upset him.

Even more interesting is the story of Mir Mehboob Ali Khan, the sixth Nizam. He had succeeded his father when he was a little over three years of age.

His teachers found it a tough ask to educate the toddler Prince. Good scholars as they were, they were required to tackle a child who, after all, held their fortunes in his tiny hands.

When the young ruler would come out, his tutor would get up and make seven salaams to him. Then, with folded hands, he would request him to take his seat so that the lessons could start. The ruler would sometimes comply, but often, when he was inclined to play, would ignore the request and run off. The tutor would follow him with folded hands. Sometimes the young ruler would not come out of the *zenana* and would start playing there. The poor teacher would keep waiting in vain outside.

The regents were hard put to find a solution to this problem. A meeting of the Regency Council was called to find a way out. After debating the issue for several days, it was decided that some children of the same age should be assembled in a class to be taught together. Whenever the little Nizam was guilty of refractory behaviour, some other child would be pulled up. Children of ordinary parents could not be given the privilege of his class-fellowship. So children of some handpicked nobles were selected for the purpose. Henceforth, whenever the Nizam refused to submit to instruction or commited some other breach of discipline, the tutor would mercilessly cane some other helpless pupil. He would cry. One of the teachers would then advise the royal student to attend to his lessons because the tutor was in a foul mood. So, until the Nizam reached adolescence, his class-fellows continued to be punished for his lapses.

Such is the etiquette to be observed before royalty. A prince's instructor can't expect to be treated as respectfully as a teacher is in the normal course. Najm, ignorant of this finer point, harboured notions of his dignity as a teacher. Once at dinner, he ticked off the Prince, saying, 'What do you know? This is an exalted position and that is the only correct view.' In spite of his exalted position, the Prince was a very cultured and large-hearted person. He looked at me and smiled at Najm's remark. I too smiled in response and the incident was ignored. But Fani remarked to me later when we were alone: 'What has happened to Najm? Does he think that the Prince is a mere schoolchild? He should simply have said, "This humble self has expressed his opinion. It is now for my Lord to decide."'

I added, 'Whenever Jaleel, the poetic preceptor of the seventh Nizam, makes any amendment in the composition of the ruler, he always writes: "The couplet of His Exalted Highness is incomparable. But in the humble opinion of this son of a slave, there is another way of putting it. It is up to my Lord and Master to choose."'

Fani said,

That is how it should be. That is why he has spent his entire life at the court. He gets a salary of Rs 1000 a month. If he were to lose his job today, can he get any job for half that amount anywhere? It is the greatness of our ruler that he pays a poet so well. How would it matter to the State if Jaleel were not there? One should know one's position and worth. Najm seems to have forgotten this axiom. I am alarmed at his tendency.

Fani often used to talk to me in this vein when we were alone. He urged me to advise Najm appropriately. He was treading a dangerous path. I always gave him same reply. I was afraid that if I ventured to advise Najm, he would think I was jealous of him and his proximity to the Prince. So I considered it prudent to keep quiet.

Shortly thereafter, another such incident took place. The Prince differed from Najm's opinion about a particular couplet. Najm was adamant and stuck to his view. The case was then sent to Jaleel, at the instance of the Prince, to elicit his opinion. The royal teacher was a discreet person. After ascertaining the Prince's opinion, he concurred with him. At dinner, the Prince alluded to it and told Fani, 'Jaleel Sahib has concurred with my view.' Najm blurted out: 'Nevertheless my opinion is correct. You may consider Jaleel's view sacrosanct, but I do not.' Everyone kept quiet. The Prince turned towards me and said, 'Obstinacy is a thing in itself.' With folded hands, I said, 'Indeed. Well said, Sire.'

Thus small incidents kept adding up. Fani and I felt apprehensive for Najm, but some of the other courtiers who were jealous of Najm's influence were happy at this development and perhaps tried to poison the Prince's mind against Najm in our absence.

If Najm had been a little cautious, nothing would have happened. Sheikh Saadi[2] has said that if during the day the king says it is night one should not only affirm it but also add that the moon and stars can be seen in the sky.

I never saw Piya differ from the Prince. If the latter had even said that Fani and Sidq deserved to be beheaded, Piya would have hailed the decision.

This in spite of the fact that Piya was fond of both of us. But he could never bring himself to differ with the Prince. Only such persons thrive in courts.

Of course, later, Piya would have placed his head at the Prince's feet and begged him to spare our lives. He would have urged him to 'forgive the trespass of the slaves. We are all transgressors, to err is in our nature and the Prince's disposition should be to overlook and to forgive it.' He would have done all that but first he would have endorsed the decision.

Nearly four years passed thus. The Prince good-naturedly kept ignoring Najm's insolence. But things were bound to come to a head. One day when the Prince was in a state of inebriation, he wanted to send a message to a guest who was staying in another bungalow. Shyam was the Comptroller of that bungalow.

The Prince asked the courtiers who should be sent on the errand. One adversary of Najm took this opportunity to suggest Najm's name. The Prince, without giving it much thought, asked his ADC to request Najm to take his message to the guest and to bring back the reply.

This was of course inappropriate and no self-respecting man would have borne the insult. But, unfortunately, at that time Najm also was in a state in which one does not think of the consequences and he didn't bother to tone down his refusal. He told the ADC curtly: 'Tell the Prince that this is not my job. He should ask me to do what I am supposed to do. For this sort of errand, Shyam or Pattan are the proper people.'

The ADC came back with Najm's reply. After a while he went to Najm again and told him that the Prince said he would pay him only Rs 150 a month as salary from that day and would also require him to run that errand. At this point, Najm lost his cool completely. Shivering with rage, he told the ADC: 'Tell the Prince that when I have declined to do such a menial job at a salary of Rs 250 a month, how can I do it at Rs 150.'

The Prince came out of his room and asked Najm angrily, 'Do you refuse to obey my orders?' Najm replied with matching vehemence: 'Absolutely,' saying which, he took off his headdress and waistband, put them on the sofa and said: 'Here is your job. I am going home.'

Najm had become a thorn in the side of some of the courtiers. That day they were elated. Fani and I felt very downcast. In our hearts, we admired Najm's courageous stand. But what worried us was the question of the sustenance of his family.

The courtiers added fuel to fire. 'It is good, Sire, that he has been removed. He composed old-style poetry.' But the Prince kept quiet on the subject for many weeks thereafter. Najm was mentioned neither in the court nor in the dining hall. It seemed as if he had never had any connection with the court.

After some months, at dinner one evening, the Prince said, 'Piya, just as the poetry of Fani and Sidq emanates from the heart, the poetry of my tutor Najm came from his head.' Piya gave his stock reply: 'Very correct, Sarkar. Your slave also thinks so. His poetry was a product of his intellect; it had nothing whatsoever to do with his emotions.'

The Prince then added: 'But his mastery was undoubted. There is no question that he was a genius.'

Piya at once changed tack. He submitted with folded hands: 'Indeed. There was no doubt about his mastery. Besides, he was knowledgeable. This slave had occasion to talk to him once or twice. He was indeed proficient in his craft. And then with four years in the company of Your Highness, he was bound to improve.'

Irani's Urdu

THE COURTIERS ALWAYS BLOW the lightest pronouncements of the Prince out of all proportion. Everybody started echoing his statement that Najm Afandi's poetry came from his head, not his heart. Unmak Jung and Dhimmak Jung, who had no knowledge of poetry, supported this view with such authority that anyone would have thought they were the Mir and Sauda.[1]

Fani and I kept quiet. The Prince also did not seem to care for our endorsement. He knew that the Hindustanis[2] were all chips of the same block. No one would speak against another.

Najm had become a recluse now. He was an ordinary citizen. That too in a strange land, a treacherous city like Hyderabad.

In a city like that, Najm lived without a job and with no means of subsistence. With a large family and his old father to support, Najm did not know what to do. The Prince owed him arrears of one year's salary but it was as good as lost. What a fall! Once his word was the Prince's command; now he could not even get to see him. Such is the way of the world.

Najm's world had changed all of sudden. He was used to going to bed at about 6.00 in the morning and getting up only at 4.00 in the afternoon. At 5.00, a car from Hill Fort would come to fetch him. He would get ready hurriedly to have tea with the Prince. Tea included a variety of delicacies and rare savouries beside seasonal and dry fruits. He would pick up bits of whatever he fancied and ignore the rest. Now his tea had only one type of biscuit, his meals consisted of only one curry—no pistachio-soup, no almond-cream pudding, no choice of curries, no rice dishes.

Like Abul Hasan,[3] he would get up to find himself in the same old house and same room, no handsome servants and no moon-faced attendants. Flabbergasted at the change of fortune, he did not know whom to turn to for help. The worst was his addiction to sleeping pills because of the Prince. Those special pills he couldn't get even on payment. Without those pills, he could not sleep and would spend the whole night pacing up and down the terrace.

Two months passed thus. After that, through the good offices of Nawab Shaheed Yar Jung 'Shaheed', one day a servant of the Prince, Habeebullah, came with a bottle of barbiturates and five notes of Rs 500 each.

With that amount, Najm paid off the arrears of his house rent, discharged the loan he had taken from Hakim Mohammad Abbas Lakhanvi, and settled the bills of Dr Akther Ahmed and Hakim Ashufta for his tonics. After some time Najm's wife's brother, Syed Ali Raza, who was Personal Assistant to the Home Secretary, Nawab Zoo-ul-Qadar Jung, and had a fair income, invited Najm and his family to stay with him. Raza lived in the compound of the home office. Najm thus moved close to me. We would spend much free time together and I kept him posted as to the goings-on at the court.

After Najm's removal, the Prince was on the lookout for a new poetic preceptor. Finally, he settled on Fani. A delegation of paid courtiers approached Fani with the offer. Fani straightaway declined it. Pressed, he replied that the Prince could hang him if he pleased but he would not accept the job. That was a mistake on Fani's part. Najm's salary was Rs 200 a month. The Prince provided dress and board. Najm also used to get Rs 40 a month by way of house rent. All this was not bad for a person who had no income. But Fani refused and, instead, proposed Shyam's name.

At dinner that evening, the Prince asked Fani, 'Do you think I am a fool?'

Astounded, Fani got up nervously, folded his hands, and replied: 'My Lord? How would I dare to even entertain such a thought?'

'Then what made you suggest the name of Shyam as my tutor?'

'Sire, his condition is pitiable because of unemployment. I thought that will give him a job.'

'His lack of employment is a different matter. First, you should have considered whether he fits the bill. I do not enjoy his dry poetry. It has no connection with heart.'

At this stage, I got up, folded my hands, and submitted: 'Nor has it anything to do with head.'

The Prince broke into laughter. Fani took advantage of his change of mood and said, 'I admit my mistake and beg your forgiveness, Sarkar.'

The Prince said, 'Correcting poetic compositions is no joke. It is a difficult job.'

Again, I interjected: 'Sire, if it was only a matter of scrutinizing poetic compositions it would be a separate issue.'

At this, the Prince laughed loud and long. All the courtiers joined him. Fani was spared further chastisement, which was my objective. Shyam was of course looking daggers at me. But I could not care less. I was enjoying my dinner.

One reason for Fani's rejection of the offer was that apart from the junior and lowly staff, no one got his salary from the Prince regularly. But this was not a valid objection. Even if it was once in six months, the salary was paid. Moreover, by accepting the job, Fani would have established a direct link with the Prince and the latter would have looked after him. But Fani lost his opportunity and I would not be surprised if he regretted it ever after.

That day an Irani gentleman was seated to my left. The Prince said, 'Sidq, This Agha [I forget the name] has been in the city for two decades and now speaks Urdu with such fluency that you will be surprised.'

I was in a mischievous mood. I stopped eating and said, 'Sarkar, No doubt your judgment is infallible, but if you permit, may I subject him to a test?'

'Of course', replied the Prince, 'examine him as you like.'

I submitted, 'Oh! I only want him to recite the following hemstitch of a couplet, My Lord:

Khaaaoon kidhar ki chot, bachaaaoon kidhar ki chot[4]

The Prince with his native intelligence immediately saw through my mischief and broke into a laugh. Fani too was beside himself with laughter. After a while, the others also understood the prank and foresaw how the Irani would play havoc with the word *chot*. The whole place reverberated with laughter. Meanwhile the Agha was looking at me with impotent rage. The Prince laughed so much that tears came into his eyes. Attendants rushed to him with hand towels. He was able to resume his dinner after quite a while.

Then he addressed Piya: 'Piya, Sidq is the life of our party.' I got up and salaamed to acknowledge the compliment. Piya praised me further. The Prince remarked, 'See, he selected such a hemstitch for testing the Agha's Urdu which is beyond the poor fellow's capacity to pronounce'. Piya said that such wit was a divine gift. Fani added, 'Sire, Sidq narrates a joke about Agha Syed Mehdi which in my view is even hotter than this.' The Prince asked me to narrate it. I protested that it would be a breach of manners to narrate that joke in such exalted company. The Prince said, 'I permit you, feel free and go ahead.'

I began:

Agha Syed Mehdi was the Collector of Raichur. He had a young man with a sense of humour on his personal staff. Anyone who wanted to see the Collector had to come through him. By chance, once a young Maratha boy met him and pleaded for a job. Looking at his innocent face, the minion thought of a prank. He told the boy: 'I will present you to the Collector, but be careful. Answer his questions in the affirmative. Otherwise you will not get a job.'

He then went to the Collector and told him that a young Maratha boy wanted to see him for a job. The Collector had just taken his evening tea and was relaxing in a mosquito net reading a newspaper. He asked him to be shown in.

The boy made his bows and stood respectfully in a corner.

The Collector asked him, 'You—Marata?'[5]

The boy, apparently stunned, retreated and replied, 'No, Sir, No. I do not want the job.'

The PA whispered to the boy: 'Say yes and you will get the job.'

The boy persisted, 'No, Sir, I don't want the job.'

The Collector was annoyed. He said, 'Whether you want the job or not is another matter, but you must answer my question.—You Marata?'

The boy retreated further and said tremulously. 'No, Sir, I won't be able to do that.' Saying so he ran away.

The Collector pulled up his PA: 'What mad dog did you bring to me? He did not reply to my question and kept on repeating himself. What did he say he would not be able to do? What was I asking him to do? Mad fellow!'

The PA apologized profusely and said that he did not know the boy had a screw loose in his head. He promised to be more careful in future.

'Poor fellow', commiserated the Agha.

Along with everybody else, now the Irani guest was also laughing. That evening, because of the jokes, dinner took a long time to finish.

⸆ When the Prince came to the hall after dinner, I was surprised to see a new person in place of the usual dancer. The new boy had a jet black face, a withered mouth, dull eyes, and long neck like a crane, yellowish teeth, small eyes, and small ears. In sheer disgust, I turned my face away from this perfect specimen of ugliness.

On the Prince's orders, instead of Moiz, that ugly creature mounted the platform. He began to recite a ghazal composed by the Prince. Fani began his rapturous exclamations. Ummak Jung and Dhimmak Jung began to jump in sycophantic ecstasy. I was sitting on the sofa, my eyes turned away from the ugly visage. Thus I had a full view of the handsome face of the Prince. By chance, the singer sang two or three couplets facing Kammo. The Prince pulled him up loudly. 'Why do you face him? Reciting to him is like playing the flute before a buffalo. Face Sidq whose reactions I want.' My misfortune! Now I had to sit facing the singer. I was wondering whether I would have to suffer his ugly face the whole night and, if so, whether I would survive till daybreak.

Then, as if aided by providence, I thought of a strategy to have him evicted from the court. Somehow, I sat through that ghazal. During the recitation of the second ghazal, on the second couplet, I cupped my hand to my left ear and turned towards Fani. This gesture was to indicate that I had not been able to hear properly the second hemistich of the couplet and wanted Fani to repeat it to me. The Prince noticed it and he himself repeated the line to me. Thereupon, I expressed my admiration appropriately. A shadow of annoyance crossed the Prince's face but it disappeared presently. After two or three minutes, I repeated the gesture, and again the Prince recited the hemstitch to me. This time the Prince's face showed signs of anger. I noted it and was pleased that my acting had not failed to bring results. A moment later, I went through the same motion again. This time the Prince lost his temper. He shouted for Moiz—who appeared nervously and stood before the Prince with folded hands. Everybody was stunned to see the Prince in that mood. A hush fell over the hall. Moiz was asked to ascend the platform and take his seat. The Prince shouted: 'Throw out that wretch. He is murdering my ghazals. Sidq is not able to hear them properly.' He was never again seen within the precincts of the Palace.

Moiz took his seat and started singing. Now I resumed my liberal and loud praise of the Prince's compositions.

Next day when Fani came to know the motive behind my acting, he was astounded. I said I could not bear to spend the night looking at that face. So I had thought of that device. Fani burst into laughter. He said he wished Josh were there. 'He would have acknowledged your cunning. You are great. May God protect you from the evil eye!'

The Deccani Colonel Blimp

ONE AFTERNOON, soon after my servant brought my tea tray Colonel G.M. Khan entered.[1] He was clad in a black sherwani and was wearing *chappals* on his feet and smiles on his face. I got up and welcomed him. The Colonel shook my hand vigorously and uttered: '*Hasbanullah naimul wakil*[2] and took a chair.

As soon as he sat down, he took upon himself the duties of host. He asked me if he could make tea for me. I said why not. Thereupon he poured tea first in my cup and then in his. Then he added sugar and milk in both the cups according to his taste. Uttering 'Hasbanullah naimul wakil' again, he then invited me to drink my tea.

The officer belonged to the old gentry of Hyderabad and hence spoke in pure Dakhni. Because of that, he stood out amongst the gentry and, in his own words, was a messenger of cheer amongst his friends and acquaintances. Let the reader too make his acquaintance.[3] His arrival was nothing short of the approach of spring.

Laughing, making others laugh, and casting horoscopes were his favourite pastimes. After school and college examinations, there would be a great rush of students to his place. Keen to know the results of their examination, they would mob him day and night. The Colonel would first get some information from the students themselves and then, on that basis, spin out some yarn to them. Or he would say: 'You are weak at maths. The rest of the subjects are all right. I fear that you might fail in maths.' To another, he would remark: 'Urdu and Persian pose a danger to your result. If you secure even pass marks in those, you'll certainly pass.' The boys were glad to hear these predictions and would rush to tell them to their parents.

One day he made the day of a rich young man by telling him that he was about to go to London. Sometimes he would forecast a pilgrimage to Mecca for some religiously inclined person. People who came to him always left dreaming of a bright future. How much of it turned out to be true, no one could say.

Generally people withdraw after retirement and become somewhat reclusive. But from the day the Colonel got his pension, he became footloose. If he returned home in the evening, it was early for him. Normally, he would seldom return before 10.00 at night.

After taking a few sips of tea, the Colonel said, 'Brother, if you promise not to mock me, I can recite some poems.' I assured him that I was eager to hear him. There was no question of laughing at him. The Colonel thereupon proceeded to recite the following trite couplet:

Taklluf se dupattaa aaj rangwaate hain woh dhaani
Khudaa jaane pade ga kis sookhe dhaan per paani

Ceremoniously, she got her scarf dyed in green
God knows whose field will green beneath her rain.

In spite of my best efforts, I could not control my laughter. The Colonel also joined me. At last, for form's sake, I said: 'Colonel Sahib, it is indeed wonderful.' The Colonel replied: 'Brother, these poets work miracles, Hasbanullah ....' I said, 'One has to applaud the masterful indirect reference in the couplet. How subtly has the poet said that she has prepared herself so well to warm the bosom of someone!'

The Colonel perhaps seeing through my mock praise said: 'Don't say that. It is the verse of some master.'

I said: 'May God bless him.'

Colonel: 'Hasbanullah ... should I proceed further?'

I said: 'Please do. Where does one get to hear such poetry?'

The Colonel then resumed:

> *Kahaa un se main, dil hai shaidaa tumhaaraá*
> *Who bole bigad kar, 'kalejaa tumhaaraa'*

> I told her my heart was sick with love for her
> She snubbed me and said it must be your liver.

I exclaimed: 'Great. These are not the opening lines of a poem but the rising of the sun. What flow! What spontaneity! The coquetry of the beloved cannot be expressed better than this. God be praised.' The Colonel asked whether he should proceed.

I asked him to repeat the lines since I hadn't quite absorbed them.

The Colonel obliged and repeated the couplet with great relish many times. I laughed to my heart's content. He then said he would go on.

'Go ahead,' I said, 'I am all ears.'

Whereupon the colonel recited:

> *Hoshyaar is qadar hoon keh kaate hain uske kaan*
> *Kooche mein tere masle-e-sag-e-dum bareeda hoon.*

> I have outsmarted him, how clever am I!
> I prowl in your street like a tailless dog.

My amusement now knew no bounds.

I expatiated on the subtle meaning of the couplet.

The faithfulness of dog is well known and the poet has included himself in that category to impress the beloved. In the first line the phrase, 'clipping the ears' is simply great. Idiomatically, it means getting the better of someone, to surpass, overcome, or outwit. The allusion is to the famous romance of the star-crossed lovers—Laila and Majnum. Laila had a dog. It is well known. If the beloved treats the lover even as a dog, he gets the privilege of lying at her door. The more you analyse the couplet, the deeper its meaning.

The Colonel was very gratified to hear my comments.

At that stage, I looked at my watch. The Colonel asked: 'What hour does your clock strike?' The Colonel used the Urdu word *ghadyal* meaning clock. He should have said *ghadi*, which means watch.

I was amused by the question. But a reply was necessary. I said, '6.30.' Then to prevent him making further forays into poetry, I asked him: 'Where have you been today?'

Colonel: 'What can I say, brother. Mr Bilgrami had been complaining for long that I had drawn the horoscope of so many people but had neglected his family. So, today I left everything and cast their horoscope, 'Hasbanullah ....'

'It was great. All of them got together and started clamouring: 'Me first, me first.' I told them not to get hassled. 'Hasbanullah ... each one can ask questions.' Time thus flew and it was half past one. Then all of them insisted that I eat there. I said, 'Why this formality.' They said there was no formality. It was my own house. When they insisted, I agreed. 'Hasbanullah ....'

'So you have had a feast?'

'Such a feast be damned. Everything was sweet, nothing salty, nothing sour, no pickles, no prawn, no fish, no curds, and no tomato. Hasbanullah ... and then, as if to needle me, they asked me to eat this sohan halwa, that burfi of the Captain's well, this royal piece, this apple jam, do eat these Colonel Sahib, do eat that. Why all this formal insistence? I got very angry but controlled myself and got up. Hasbanullah ....'

My sides were splitting. I beseeched him not to give further details of the feast lest I should die of laughter. The Colonel felt very happy and in the same mood, proceeded to tell the story of the late Nawab Shahab Jung. In his childhood, he used to live beside the female quarters of the Nawab. But I will stop trying to reproduce the Colonel's style and language and I will revert to my own style of narration.

Nawab Shahab Jung

NAWAB SHAHAB JUNG was a respected noble of the period of the sixth Nizam, Mir Mehboob Ali Khan. He was the son of the sister of Sir Salar Jung I, the great Diwan of Hyderabad for thirty years from 1853. He was Minister for Police under the sixth Nizam. His personal loyalty to the Nizam had added to his pedigree. People respected him and the ruler was kind to him. The female quarters of his mansions were close to the royal seraglio.

Since evening, his servants would get busy lighting up hundreds of candles and lamps from the female quarters to the drawing room of the building. There were two costly chandeliers in his drawing room. Each one had thirty-two lotuses inlaid with gold and silver. They cast so much light that night seemed like day. Then there were numerous smaller lights all around. The reason for such lavish lighting was that Shahab Jung did all his work—whether official or private—at night. He met his callers, gave instructions to the managers of his estates, and held out hopes to the job seekers only at night. Letters were answered and decisions pronounced only at that time. The Commissioner of Police gave his reports of the day to him and received further instructions in the dead of night. His office and his personal staff were used to spend the night working.

There was such a rush of people—applicants, respondents, lawyers, job seekers—that the compound gave the impression of a fair. Petty shopkeepers had opened scores of shops in the compound to cater to the requirements of the people. But the thing for which Shahab Jung became a legend was the row of servants from his office hall to the private apartments. These liveried attendants changed duty every two or three hours but the row remained intact till early morning. This platoon was not for mere show. They served a purpose which no one before or since Shahab Jung had ever thought of. I have not heard of such an arrangement even for rulers. They were there to meet the needs of the nobleman during the night. If, for example, he felt thirsty while at work, he would ask his orderly for water. The orderly would open the door and shout for water. This order would be relayed through the human chain to the last man. Just as boys play volleyball, or a particular line is 'lifted' by the audience in mushairas, the order for water would travel from mouth-to-mouth and finally reach the pantry. The man-in-charge would fill a silver tumbler with water, put it on a silver tray, and pass it on to the man next to him. This tray would then be relayed back from servant to servant along with a loud declaration by each: 'Water is hereby served.' Finally, the orderly would, in the same singsong manner in which he was used to calling the parties to court, announce the arrival of water and present the tray to the Nawab with a bow. His announcement would wake up the lawyers who would be dozing outside the office.

After a while, Shahab Jung would ask for a paan. The same drill was repeated and this time the demand would be relayed to the private apartments where a lady would prepare his special paan and relay it back to the lord and master. Then a demand for a cigar would be fulfilled through the same elaborate procedure. This commotion would continue from 11.00 at night to 5.00 in the morning.

According to Piya, one night at about 2.00, the late Nizam Mahboob Ali Khan went up to his terrace to enjoy the cool quiet night. There he heard, 'Water is hereby presented' being repeated endlessly into the otherwise silent night. The Nizam asked Piya what the tumult was about. Before he could say anything, a noble, Nawab Shamsher Jung, submitted with folded hands, 'Your Highness, Nawab Shahab Jung must have asked for water. Water is being carried for him and this commotion is because of the announcement regarding the gradual and serial compliance of his orders.' The Nizam just smiled and kept quiet.

One evening when Nawab Shahab Jung was in attendance, the Nizam remembered the other night's commotion. He addressed the Nawab: 'Shahab Jung, because of the din and pother in your mansion throughout the night, I cannot sleep. Why don't you change your residence so that I can sleep in peace?'

Shahab Jung submitted with folded hands, 'This slave of Your Highness has only one humble abode. If he leaves it, where will he take shelter? My Lord, on the other hand, has scores of places. If this servant of his was in that position, he would have instantly complied with the orders of His Highness.' The subtle hint was that changing the residence was no problem for the Nizam. So why shouldn't he shift rather than ask the Nawab to do so. The Nizam was a kind ruler. He simply smiled at the retort. This incident shows how close the Nawab was to the Nizam and how much of his confidence he enjoyed.

There are two more incidents relating to Nawab Shahab Jung worth narrating. They give an idea of his prestige and self-esteem.

A meeting of a committee of the nobles of the State held to sort out an important matter was to be chaired by the Nizam. At the last moment, however, the Nizam was unable to do so. But he did not want the meeting to be postponed. So he deputed his Chief Secretary, Moulvi Ahmed Hussain, to attend the meeting and to make a report to him for a decision. The Moulvi went to the meeting, informed all members of the committee of the Nizam's orders, and took the chair.

Thereupon Nawab Shahab Jung got up and said it was impossible that during his lifetime a paid servant of the State should preside over a meeting of a committee of nobles. Turning to the Chief Secretary, he said: 'This committee comprises all the leading nobles of the State. Will you decide the fate of such people? You may be getting a salary of Rs 3000 or 5000 but you are nevertheless an employee.' The Chief Secretary protested that he was representing the Nizam under his orders. Shahab Jung said he would take it upon himself to answer the Nizam but that the Chief Secretary should go away.

Ahmed Hussain reported the incident to the Nizam probably with some exaggeration. The Nizam was infuriated. He asked the delinquent Nawab to be presented before him at once. He was duly brought in. The Nizam asked the Nawab in great anger: 'What is this, Shahab Jung? You did not care for my orders and sent back my representative!'

Shahab Jung folded his hands and submitted, 'My Lord, that committee consisted of all the nobles of Hyderabad. How could this slave allow the indignity of letting a paid employee sit amongst them?'

The Nizam said, 'The nobles are all my creatures. I can put my foot on anyone's head.'

The Nawab persisted, 'This humble servant is fully aware of that. But My Sovereign, the only fit place for your shoe is the head of Shahab Jung. You can't place it anywhere else?'

The Nizam cooled down and smiled. The Nawab returned home triumphant.

The second incident is even more interesting. Once the Nawab was annoyed with Akbar Jung, the *Kotwal* (the Commissioner of Police of the city), about some matter. He imposed a fine of Re 1 on him. Akbar Jung was naturally very upset at such humiliation. He appealed to the Nizam against the punishment. When Shahab Jung went to pay his respects to the Nizam, the latter told him that the Kotwal was his trusted servant. 'You have imposed a fine of Re 1 on such a person!' Shahab Jung said he would reconsider the matter. Returning to his office, he recalled the file and wrote on it: 'Half the fine remitted. Let him pay only 8 annas (half a rupee).'

And the highest police officer of the city, getting a salary of Rs 2000 a month, had to pay that fine!

Shahab Jung basked in the reflected glory of the Nizam. But alas, as often happens in this world, his pre-eminence did not last, After the death of Nizam Mehboob Ali Khan, the Nawab so fell from favour[1] that he withdrew from public life and never showed his face to anyone. He only emerged from his mansion again enclosed in a coffin. His historic mansion where nights were brighter than days is in such a dilapidated state that one feels heartsick just talking about it.

One evening in 1953, Syed Barkat Ali, a *jagirdar*, and Khwaja Moinuddin together showed me the ruins of that mansion. The Khwaja was the guide and he pointed out: 'This was his office, this the verandah in which the supplicants thronged; this was where drinking water was kept; these were the female quarters; this was his dressing room; this was where his visitors waited; this was the dining hall; this is where he said his prayers.' The roof had collapsed in most places. Only some pillars stood in their lonely glory. I cannot express my feelings after seeing the ruins. I wanted to embrace those pillars and cry. Ah, the evanescence of glory! Everything looked empty and meaningless to me. The high and the mighty with whom I mixed daily now appeared mere clowns. In that introspective and reflective mood, I composed a poem.

The car from the Hill Fort pulled up in front of my house. Fani was already sitting in it. Colonel Khan got up to take leave of me. Then he put his hands in his pocket and said: 'God! What cold. Hasbanullah ....'

'Khuda Hafiz,' I said, 'God be with you.'

'Khuda Hafiz,' and he was off.

In a hurry, I forgot to take my *paandan* with me. When I sat down for dinner with the Prince, I remembered it. But I had to suffer in silence. After dinner, the Prince very kindly offered me a paan. I applied some tobacco to it and, putting it in my mouth, thanked the great provider. When Moiz started singing, I got so lost in his magical voice that I did not think of the packet of paan which I had left behind at home. But it was my practice that as soon as the Prince looked away, I would hurriedly put a paan in my mouth. So, my hand kept on going to my pocket from sheer force of habit. As I took my empty hand from my pocket, the Prince realized my problem. He asked loudly: 'What is the matter today? Sidq is not chewing.'

I got up and replied with folded hands: 'Sarkar, unfortunately I forgot to bring my paan container today.' He said that Fani could help me out. Thereupon Fani got up and said that he too had forgotten to bring his packet. The Prince began to laugh at this coincidence. He then beckoned an attendant and asked him to bring two hundred betel leaves from his stock along with ground tobacco in a bottle and to put them between Fani and me so that we could resume our 'mastication'.

Both of us got up and did seven grateful salaams. I thought it would take at least half-an-hour before the paans would materialize. But to our surprise the attendant brought two hundred paans arranged neatly in a silver tray in no time and placed them between us. We again got up and made our salaams. But the Prince did not tell us to eat the paans and to eat anything without his permission was against court etiquette.

Those who are addicted to tobacco can imagine our plight. It was as if a glass of water was within reach of a thirsty person but he was not allowed to drink it. Thus helpless, time passed and soon it struck 3.00. Then the Prince himself turned towards his bedroom, and we picked up two paans each.

Fani said, 'I wish we had our paan-boxes. Then we could have filled them with these special paans.' I replied that if we had the boxes, we would not even have seen the special paans. Fani began to laugh and said that the Prince had put us to a severe test and thanks to God, we had emerged successful. 'He wanted to see whether the "foreigners" are worthy of the honour bestowed upon them.' He again began to thank God for saving our honour. But before he could finish, the handsome dancer boy came and stood beside me. I offered him two paans. He accepted them with a smile and then asked me to repeat a particular couplet, which he said he liked very much. I obliged him readily:

> *Yeh baat bigadne ki nahin jis peh khafaa ho*
> *Detaa hai Khudaa husn to padti hai nazar bhi*

> Do not be cross; there is nothing to mind
> When God gives beauty, all eyes turn towards it.

'What a lovely couplet,' he observed, 'I shall never forget it.' Fani remarked, 'Why forget? It is worth remembering.' The lad laughed at this and said, 'It has exquisite simplicity. It makes it seem that composing poetry is very easy. Anybody can do it.' Fani remarked: 'That is the difficult thing, very difficult.'

After that, we lit a cigarette each and chatting with each other, went out of the hall. Outside, a row of cars were lined up. The young man had to go in a different car. He shook my hand and, by way of goodbye, said, 'Khuda Hafiz'—God be with you.

I replied, 'Sorry, I can't entrust you to God.'

'Why,' he asked.

I recited this couplet in reply:

> *Yeh rashk badi balaa hai dam-e-rukhsat-e-habib*
> *Kyonkar kahoon Khuda hai nigehbaan—jaaiye*
>
> Ah, damned jealousy! When parting,
> I can't entrust my beloved even to God.

Fani praised the couplet. That boy too liked it and noted it down in his scrapbook.

From the Hill Fort to Abid Road, where I stayed, was a drive of five minutes. As soon as the state car entered my compound, my dogs leapt at me. Each wanting to engage my attention, Fanny and Tommy started a bout amongst themselves. Fani enjoyed the dog fight and for weeks after kept describing it to friends. Tommy was a brave dog. He would take on any cat and hound it to death. Three months after killing his ninth cat, he died following a short illness. The vet in the main hospital tried to save him and gave him a number of injections but his efforts were in vain. I buried him near the Polo Ground under a neem tree.

I was so grief stricken at his death that I did not attend Court for three days. Fani and Najm came daily to console me. Josh sent me a telegram of condolence:

'Read in the daily *Payam* death of Mr Tommy. Sincere condolences. I share your sorrow in this bereavement as deceased was also my intimate friend.

Sogwar [grieving] Josh

A Mullah who was teaching ethics in a middle school in Parbani wrote a letter to me criticizing my excessive attachment to the dog. It was full of nonsense. I simply sent him a couplet in reply:

Ai nafse-e-khabis, aadmi ban
Kutte main vali ki khaslaten hain

Oh soul of Satan, become a man
Dogs have the qualities of saints!

Whenever I had sat with my friends in the drawing room, Tommy would come and jump onto his chair like a prince. This chair had been set apart for him to my friends' astonishment. Now, whenever I saw the vacant chair, I was overcome by emotion. I relieved my feelings somewhat by writing a poem on him.

Royal Largesse

ON FANI'S INSISTENCE, I attended Court on the fourth day. The Prince asked me why I had been absent for three days. I replied that I had not been well.

That day, after the soup, the first dish placed before the Prince was *khichidi*.[1] The Prince helped himself to many spoonfuls and ate with relish. After that, he asked for it to be placed before me. I got up and made seven salaams for this special favour. However, I took only one spoonful so that I could eat some *pilav* later. After I had helped myself, the Prince ordered it to be served to Fani. Like me, Fani also, treating it as an inferior dish, took only one spoonful. But as soon as I put the spoon in my mouth, I realized my mistake. I had never in my life enjoyed biryani or pilav as much as this seemingly ordinary dish. Now I did not want to touch anything else. But it was too late. Fani also regretted his disdain for khichidi. I do not know whether subsequently he got it in heaven, but in this world, it is not easy to come by such a delicacy. I learnt that peeled almonds were sliced so finely that they couldn't be told apart from grains of rice. Similarly, pistachio nuts were sliced finely to mingle with *mash daal* (a variety of pulses). The sliced almonds and pistachios were mixed with rice and daal in equal measure and the concoction cooked on slow fire. I could not ascertain whether ghee was mixed in equal or double proportion. Every type of pilav now appeared worthless before this khichidi.

The Prince ate figs after dinner. He did not touch any other fruit. The basket of fruit was kept for mere decoration and was probably polished off by the servants later. The Prince would throw one fig each to Fani and me. Piya, Carew, Ummak Jung, and Dhimmak Jung were also included in the favour.

That day, I don't know what came upon Kammo. Before the Prince could turn to the bowl of figs, Kammo extended his hand and helped himself to one. It was a serious breach of etiquette and the Prince was visibly annoyed. He asked the attendant to place the whole bowl before Kammo who, taking it as a favour, started salaaming the Prince with both hands. The Prince looked at me and smiled. I too smiled at the simpleton. It was a practice with the Asaf Jahi rulers and princes that if anyone touched anything belonging to them, it was given away to that person. They never used it again themselves.

During the reign of the sixth Nizam, Mehboob Ali Khan, once while a sweeper was sweeping the floor of his bedroom, he saw a beautiful shining object on a side-table. He picked it up and was looking at it in wonder, when suddenly the Nizam appeared. The sweeper began trembling with fear and was about to replace the object, when the Nizam remarked to the sweeper: 'Now it belongs to you'. The shocked sweeper bent double to thank him and put the cigarette holder in his pocket.

.   Thereafter the sweeper began to use the costly holder to smoke his cheap cigarettes. Some time later the Nizam went on a visit to Bombay. The sweeper also went as a part of his retinue. The Nizam stayed at the Taj Hotel for two weeks. During this period, the sweeper formed a friendship with a bearer of the hotel. The sweeper was a simpleton who didn't realize that with the Nizam's gift, he was no longer poor. He could, if he wanted, live the rest of his life in ease and comfort by selling the diamond studded holder. On the other hand, the bearer was a shrewd, cunning fellow. He realized that the sweeper was unaware of the value of the cigarette holder. On the day of the Nizam's departure, the bearer threw a party for him, as if bidding farewell to a dear friend. After that, he came to the point. 'Friend,' he said sentimentally, 'one does not know when we will meet again. If you do not mind, I would like to have your cigarette holder as a keepsake. It will remind me of you whenever I smoke.' The simple sweeper gladly gave away the holder to his newfound friend.

The bearer rushed to a jeweller to sell the holder. The jeweller valued it at Rs 1,50,000, but, suspecting that it might have been stolen and fearing that he might land himself in trouble, he informed the police. The Bombay Police concluded that it must belong to the Nizam of Hyderabad. The statement of the accused was recorded and, holding him in custody, the police sent an officer to Hyderabad to make further investigations. The matter was reported to the Nizam through the Commissioner of Police. He was told that a bearer of the Taj Hotel in Bombay claimed that a cigarette holder had been given to him by a sweeper of His Highness as a parting gift. The Nizam recalled that he had indeed given his sweeper a cigarette holder. The sweeper confirmed that he had given it to the bearer of his own will. The Bombay Police was accordingly informed. The bearer was released and became a rich man. The sweeper continued in his lowly job.

After dinner, there was a sitting in the Darbar Hall. Nawab Qudrat Nawaz Jung made a paan from his own paan-box, got up, and presented it submissively to the Prince. Then he took one himself. The Prince was at that time talking to me. Suddenly, I noticed that the Nawab whispered something into Piya's ear. Piya nodded. The Nawab then went to Fani and whispered something to him. I thought it must be about some special matter concerning the court. I didn't realize that a conspiracy was being hatched against me.

After whispering to Fani, the Nawab went and stood respectfully by the Prince's side. When the Prince looked up, he folded his hands and made a submission: 'Sire, this slave has been keen for a long time to hear one of Sidq's poems. If Your Lordship permits, an old wish of mine will be fulfilled.' Before the Prince could say anything, Piya and Fani also got up with folded hands and seconded the Nawab's proposal. The Prince asked: 'Which poem is this? Tell me something about it before I ask him to oblige.' Fani said: 'Sarkar, It lampoons a professor of Delhi.' The Prince asked in surprise: 'So Sidq's talents run in that direction also?' Fani replied: 'He is a master in that genre. There is hardly a noble in Hyderabad who has not held special feasts in order to hear this particular poem.' The Prince said: 'Then let me also arrange a feast first. If he recites it only at feasts, why should I be guilty of breaking the rule?'

I got up with folded hands and said: 'I enjoy feasts here every day. My Lord does not have to do anything more. The Prince replied: 'What you eat daily here is only pot-luck.' I submitted: 'Any noble will gladly exchange a feast with such a pot-luck, Sarkar.' The Prince laughed at this and then asked Fani for the background to the lampoon so that he could enjoy it fully.'

Fani: 'Huzur, the professor tried to give one of Ghalib's[2] couplets a new interpretation. The Prince then asked me for the details.

I submitted:

My Lord, he is a perverted person. In his arrogance, he calls Moulvi Abdul Haq a mere student and refers to Tabatabai and Jaleel with contempt. One day he said to me that Ghalib was introduced to the world by his pupil, Hali.[3] If he had not written *Yadgar-e-Ghalib*, nobody would have known Ghalib today. But there were couplets of Ghalib which even Hali could not understand.

When I asked him to give an example, he recited the following couplet:

> *Karte ho mujh ko manaa kadam bosi ke liye*
> *Kyaa aasmaan ke bhi baraabar nahin hoon main?*

> You forbid me from kissing your feet.
> Am I not equal even to Aasmaan [sky]?

Then he said that if anyone amongst Abdul Haq, Tabatabai, or Jaled could explain the couplet, he would become their slave. To establish oneself amongst the ignorant by growing a long beard was one thing; to acquire solid knowledge is another.

The Prince asked: 'To whom does the allusion of growing a beard apply?'

'Moulvi Abdul Haq, Sire,' I replied.

I then proceeded.

I then requested him to expatiate on the couplet. He extracted a promise from me that I would not divulge it to Abdul Haq, Tabatabai, or Jaleel. Otherwise, they would appropriate it. He then gave a fantastic interpretation of the couplets.

Ghalib had a liaison with a prostitute. She had a young servant called Aasmaan [which means sky]. The poet has played on the meaning of his name to make a point. He says, 'The boy presses your feet every morning. And I, your lover, am prevented form kissing them. Am I not equal status even to this servant of yours—Aasmaan?'

After this explanation, he looked triumphantly at me. He said there were scores of such couplets, which he could explain to the so-called learned trio as he did to his students.

The Prince asked me, laughing, how I'd reacted.

I expressed my contempt for the Professor's 'learning'. The Prince then asked me to recite the lampoon.

I then recited the long poem which took me two hours to complete because I had to repeat each couplet many times. Everybody liked the poem, and each one praised it in his own way.[4] The Prince commented that the poem constituted a very valuable addition to Urdu literature.

Fani termed any unusual happening in the court as an 'accident'. That week, in his words, two 'accidents' occurred. One was that the handsome dancer happened somehow to earn the displeasure of the Prince. Fani, who was good at investigating such matters, tried his best to discover the cause but was unable to do so.

The second 'accident' related to Moiz. He used to sport a 4-inch long beard, which suited him well. Suddenly one day he appeared clean-shaven. He looked funny in the beginning but gradually we got used to the new look.

Fani, during one of our strolls, told me that the dancer's beard was forcibly removed on the orders of the Prince who did not like it. He had asked Moiz many times to shave it off but Moiz considered it a sign of manhood and a gift of God and would not oblige. One evening eight attendants took hold of Moiz and held him down, while a barber cleared the 'hedge'.

I asked Fani what compensation the Prince had paid Moiz for the loss.

'Nothing,' replied Fani. I said, 'That was not fair of the Prince. He should have paid Rs 2000 by way of compensation. That would have mollified Moiz. A small charity was called for.' Fani replied, 'In that case you would have started keeping a beard and then Mahirul Qadri would have followed suit. The Prince would then have been entangled in a web of beards.' 'That would have been no big deal for him. After all, remember he is the grandson of the Great Generosity personified,' I said. Fani looked around to ensure no one was within earshot and then whispered, 'You look too far; you don't see the wood for the trees. Don't you know whose son he is?' Saying this Fani broke into a guffaw. I said, 'His father was also the son of that grandfather. The only difference is that the old man was a spendthrift and our present ruler is provident. He doesn't squander money lest he should, like his father, have to borrow from the government ....'

At this point a handsome attendant came running and informed us that the Prince had come into the hall and we should make haste to return. We complied.

The Departure of Begum Akhtar

AKHTAR BAI OF FAIZABAD who had been the Prince's guest for two weeks at Rs 2000 a day was about to leave. That night was her last singing session.

Lest readers wonder that I have talked of the renowned singer only on the last day of her visit, let me explain that she was a woman of very ordinary looks. Her voice was divine but because of her plain looks I don't consider her colourful enough to adorn too many pages of my account of a very colourful court.

At 2.00 in the morning, the Prince asked her to sing a *thumri*.[1] She was tuning her instruments. Her voice was so melodious that one could not distinguish between her voice and the notes of the *sarangi*.[2] God! What a voice she had. The Prince startled me by addressing me: 'Sidq, you see! You can't make out the notes of sarangi from her voice.' I replied that I had been thinking the same. The Prince had taken the words from my mouth. 'What a coincidence!' remarked the Prince.

As usual, the session broke up at 3.00 in the morning. We were all permitted to leave. We had just got into the car when an attendant came running and said that the Prince wanted me. Fani was allowed to go home. I followed the attendant to the terrace of the Palace. The floor was covered with a large cotton carpet. The Prince was sitting on a chair. I made the prescribed bows. The Prince said, 'Sidq, so, little of the night is left that it would be an insult to it to let it pass in sleep. That is why I called you back. Go only after having breakfast with me.' I responded with folded hands, 'Very good idea, Huzur. To think of sleep now is to get condemned on the Day of Judgment. Poor Fani.' The Prince laughed at this for some time and then seconded me: 'Poor Fani, indeed.' Then he turned to an attendant: 'Take a car at once. Go to Banjara Hills and fetch Akhtari. If she has gone to bed, wake her up. Tell her this is my order. There should not be even a second's delay.' The servant bowed and rushed out. The Prince then ordered another attendant: 'Bring the gifts we are going to give to Akhtari on her departure.' The servant bowed and went to the wardrobe. Presently Akhtari entered and made her salaams. The Prince said to her: 'Soon it will be morning. I think to lie down and sleep at this time ...' I cut in, '... would be to forgo the merit of a vigil.' The Prince laughed at this interjection. Akhtari joined in. Meanwhile the attendants started spreading the gifts in front of us. There were twelve saris in twelve silver trays. Every sari had a costly blouse-piece to match. Each sari was worth a thousand rupees. There was a tape cot, each leg of which was made of silver. There was a silver filigree stand for a goblet with a silver tumbler. Then there were a paandan, a scent-box, and a spittoon—all in silver. Last of all was a costly wristwatch. The attendants spread out all these things like the dowry of a rich bride on display.

The Prince said, 'Sidq, these small gifts are presented to Akhtari on my behalf.' Akhtari got up and salaamed. I said one should swear by the guest towards whom the Prince was so kindly disposed.

The Prince said: 'Selecting the gifts was not difficult. But getting the blouses to match the saris was not an easy job.' I submitted, 'Your choice, My Lord, is indeed apt. God has indeed blessed you with special talents. Every blouse matches its sari like a precious stone in a ring.' The Prince was pleased with this praise. Probably he had detained me for just that reason. He said, 'Good, I am now satisfied. I admire your taste.' I got up and salaamed in grateful acknowledgement of the compliment.

Then the Prince said, 'See, if I had given Akhtari in cash what I have spent on these gifts, she would probably have been happier. But whatever I want to give, I give by way of gifts, not cash. I don't know why.' 'I understand, Sir,' I said. The Prince asked me to explain. I folded my hands and submitted. 'A gift of cash demeans the recipient. He feels embarrassed. Sarkar wants the recipient to be spared that awkwardness. This shows Your Lordship's graciousness.' The Prince said, 'Well, it is for you to judge.' Akhtari looked at me in surprise.

The Prince then turned to Akhtari: 'I want you to eat something now. What would you like?' Akhtari folded her hands and pointing to her throat said, 'Whatever I have eaten is still stuck here. I could not even sleep because of over-eating. So Your Highness, there is no question of eating anything more.' The Prince said authoritatively: 'Eat you must because I feel like that. However, I allow you choice of the item.' Akhtari was cleverer and shrewder than most women of her profession generally are. She reflected for a moment and then said, 'If the Prince insists, I will eat pineapple *murabba* [a sort of Indian jam].' My heart started pounding. I prayed to God to save the Prince's honour. Where would he procure jam at 4.00 in the morning? I angrily prayed to God to save people from women of Akhtari's profession. But the Prince seemed unperturbed. He turned to an attendant and asked him to bring pineapple jam. The servant said 'Yes, Sire', bowed, and vanished. After a few minutes, I was surprised to see the same attendant returning, followed by five hefty men holding a glass jar each. I had never seen such big jars before. Every jar was full of pineapple jam. There must have been 12 kilos of jam in each jar.

My surprise knew no bounds. I said to myself: 'He is indeed a Prince. Most rulers would have failed such a test.'

Akhtari had thought that she had asked for the impossible. She must have been sure that her demand could not be fulfilled and the Prince would be defeated. But now she too was taken aback. A servant placed a plate and spoon in front of her. With an uncertain hand, she forked out half-a-piece and put it in her plate. I am sure she must not have eaten such tasty jam before. But she refrained from praising it lest she should have to eat more.

Attendants cleared the table. The Prince then gave instructions about the gifts. 'Pack them properly in a suitcase and tomorrow when she boards the train, put the suitcase by her side. Show her everything so that nothing is left out due to oversight.' Thereupon Akhtari got up and salaamed the Prince. He asked her to go and have a wash. 'It is now close to breakfast time.'

Akhtari proceeded towards the toilet. The Prince summoned his ADC, Razvi, and instructed him: 'In the morning when Akhtari goes to the bazaar, you be with her. All her shopping will be on my account.'

It was about 4.30 in the morning when the Prince ordered breakfast. A small table was laid for four. The fare was very simple—just *nahari* (a meat dish with soup), and *sheermal* (round baked bread with milk). But when sheermal is made only of milk, clarified butter, and resin, it is unimaginably delicious. The nahari was also better than any I had even eaten.

Breakfast was over at 6.00 and we were permitted to leave. I took casual leave from my school that day and slept till 1.00 in the afternoon.

At 4.00 in the evening, I went to Fani's house. I saw him making complicated calculations on a sheet of paper. I asked him whether he was calculating his debts. Fani replied, 'No this is some other account.' Then he added: 'Our ruler, the Nizam has established Trusts for the two Princes. Each Trust will consist of around Rs 2,57,66,000.[3] I was computing the income from the trust, which our Prince will get. I said, 'Whatever be the amount, how does it concern you?'

Fani replied: 'We *are* concerned. See, now the Prince gets an allowance of Rs 25,000 a month. That is not enough to meet his expenses. Money is always tight. How can he give anything to people like you and me? But when the trust comes into existence, his monthly income will run into hundreds of thousands. Then he will be more considerate to us. Now he is helpless. Whatever he gets is filched by his hangers-on and entertainers. He finds it difficult to manage within the amount. How can he look after us?' The whole evening was spent in the calculation. While doing so, Fani took into account the rate of interest of the best banks in the world. At that time neither he nor I knew that by the time the Prince would really become a prince by virtue of the trust, so much would have changed. Real wealth is one's good deeds. Ah, the ambitions of men! They only turn to dust!

Ragging Piya

ONE NIGHT AT COURT, around 1.00 a.m., which was the time for dance, the absence of the handsome dancer was acutely felt. The Prince ordered that Carew be woken up and produced before him. Within ten minutes, Carew was standing there, making his salutations. An old man of 80 years, he was quite cross at having been woken up at that unearthly hour.

The Prince said, with considerable affection, 'Come, Carew. I have bothered you at this late hour. But circumstances were such that I had to do so.' Carew asked, alarmed, 'I hope everything is alright, My Lord?' The Prince replied: 'If everything was alright, why would I have bothered you?' Turning towards Piya, he said, 'Look at him. He does not seem at all well. Seems to be on his last breath.' Piya, who did not like any reference to impending death, was annoyed. He protested: 'This slave is alright. Please don't say anything inauspicious, Sire.' The Prince asked Carew: 'What do you, think? Is he really alright, as he says?' Carew replied, looking intently at Piya's face: 'His face looks pale and funereal. I wonder if he will survive.' Piya said angrily, 'May your face reflect death.' Then turning to the Prince

he said, 'Let him jabber, My Lord, this slave of yours is absolutely alright.'
Carew said: 'My Lord, shall I recite *Sura-e-Yaseen*[1]?'

Piya retorted angrily: 'Recite it for your near and dear ones. What is
this nonsense?'

The Prince told an attendant: 'Ring up Colonel Waghray.[2] Whoever
picks up the phone, tell him to ask the doctor to come here immediately.
There is a serious case for him to examine.' Poor Piya insisted: 'God forbid,
Sire. Your slave is fit and fine. Please don't say anything ill-omened.'

After fifteen minutes, Colonel Waghray entered and made his salaams
to the Prince.

The Prince told him: 'Waghray. Just examine Piya and tell me how
long he is likely to survive.' Waghray took one look at Piya and said gravely:
'Sire, what is left in him now? I give him two hours at the most.' Piya said
helplessly: 'You are talking rot. You will die within two hours. I shall yet
live for a long time.' The Prince ignored him and said: 'Waghray, will you
be able to treat and save him or shall I ask Carew to start reciting *Sura-e-
Yaseen?*' Waghray shook his head and said: 'In my view the time for treatment
is over. It is better to read the *sura*.'

Piya said with annoyance: 'A hale and hearty person cannot be treated.
But you should get your head examined by some other physician.' Carew
said: 'In my humble opinion, Sire, let us try fanning him with the Quran.
Maybe the Great Physician will cure him.

Piya was incensed: 'What rot you are talking in this exalted court.'
Turning to the Prince, he said: 'Sarkar, I am reminded of a couplet. With
your permission, I will recite it:

> *Quran ki havaa dene peh ahbaab musir hain*
> *Main keh nahin saktaa tere daaman ki havaa ho*

> They are bent on fanning me with the Quran
> I cannot say I'd rather have it from your scarf.'

The Prince was immensely pleased to hear this. He made Piya repeat it
many times. Looking towards Fani, he praised it. Fani endorsed the Prince's
acclamation. The practical joke with Piya ended on this note.

Thus there was a certain refinement about the Prince's court. There
was a decent limit up to which practical jokes could be stretched so that no
cultured person take objection or feel hurt. In my youth in UP, I moved in
the best circles in Lucknow. I came across first-class connoisseurs of literature

and aesthetes but the truth is that none was as good as Prince Muazzam Jah or Maharaja Kishen Pershad. The Maharaja is no more and I have no connection with the Prince now. So there is no question of flattery. I write only the truth.

Next day when, as usual, I reached the Hill Fort along with Fani, I was surprised that the courtiers were talking very freely. I learnt that the Prince had gone somewhere and was not expected back before 9.30 p.m.

After a while, an attendant brought a round teapoy and placed it in front of Fani and me. Then he brought some melons in a tray from the refrigerator. He cut them into two cups, removed their seeds, filled the cups with cream, put each half on a beautiful plate, and placed one in front of each. I looked in surprise at him. He smiled and requested us to eat them. To enable us to do so he put a spoon in each plate. Fani asked him whether the Prince had left instructions to the effect. He smiled and, shaking his head in the negative, said, 'No, I am offering you this hospitality on my own.' I asked him the reason. He replied, 'I am an admirer of your poetry.' I commented that he looked educated. He said that he had appeared in the High School examinations but unfortunately did not pass. We ate the melons to please him. That fruit from the Prince's table, that special cream, cooled in the royal refrigerator, tasted heavenly. He gave us another helping. I don't remember his name. May God keep him happy!

The Prince returned at 9.30 sharp. The chat that ensued was interesting. To use Fani's term, another 'accident' occurred that day. It was about 2.00 in the morning. Moiz was singing one of the ghazals of the Prince. Everybody was exclaiming ecstatically when suddenly the Prince shouted sternly: 'Rub the other eye also.' I looked towards where his eyes were turned and I saw Mahirul Qadri rubbing his eyes with both hands. I smiled and turned back to look at Moiz. There was a superstition in the Asaf Jahi dynasty that rubbing only one eye was inauspicious. There was, therefore, an order to the effect that if anyone needed to rub his eye, he should rub both at the same time. Mahir had, because of some irritation, rubbed only one eye by mistake. It was his good luck that it happened in the court of the Prince. Had it been in that of the Nizam, all hell would have broken loose. During my stay of a quarter of a century in Hyderabad, how many people suffered because of this small lapse! One person was thrown out of the mosque at the time of the Friday sermon of the Imam; another humiliated in the court, yet another cast out of a gathering to celebrate the Prophet's birthday. Mahir looked sheepish at that snub.

That evening we learnt that the Prince would be going to Paris on holiday during the coming summer. Fani was relieved to hear that. He said to me, 'Good. We will have a reprieve for three months. The simple fare of our homes is better than the delicacies of this Palace. We will be masters of our nights and days.' I replied, 'Certainly, it would be better, provided we could get almonds and pistachios with the cream of Hill Fort.' Fani said, 'No chance. Those are compensations for our vigils and our hard labour as royal companions.'

The Prince Goes to Europe

THE FOLLOWING NIGHT, which should be called the last night of the season, a young man of about 27, Multani by name, mounted the dais and started dancing. The occasional exclamations of praise by the Prince were enthusiastically seconded by Ummak Jung and Dhimmak Jung. I myself found that one hour of dance very boring. I kept on smoking cigarette after cigarette. I learnt that the hideous-looking young man was a replacement for the earlier moon-faced dancer. That made the duration even more torturous.

The Prince seemed to guess that I did not like the show. But he kept quiet. Early in the morning, at about 3.00, when everybody had bid farewell to the Prince, he asked me to stay back. He took me to an open terrace of the palace, where his baggage for the trip to Europe was being packed. The attendants quickly put two chairs there. I glanced at the paraphernalia spread out there. There were about 150 elegant walking sticks, about 200 pairs of the best English shoes, countless pairs of socks, thousands of exquisitely tailored suits, and rows of neckties.

'You must be wondering', said the Prince to me, 'why I have brought you to a junkyard. But I wanted you to have a look at the baggage I am carrying with me. Besides, I wanted to talk to you.'

'At your service, Sire,' I said, 'please continue the inspection of your baggage.' My mind, meanwhile, jumped to the final journey. Would those who felt the need for so much paraphernalia on their worldly trips find it more difficult to go empty-handed to eternity? I felt a shiver run through my body at the thought. I prayed to God to forgive my sins. The Prince broke into my reverie and said, 'You come to the Begumpet[1] station to bid me goodbye. There will be too many people at Nampally. Tell Fani also to come'. I said both of us would be there.

The rest of the night was spent in small talk. I returned home after breakfast. Before going to sleep, I wrote a note to Colonel G.M. Khan telling him that I would be at his house at around 4.00 p.m. and that he should wait for me, and also that since he wished to have a close look at the Prince, the station at which the latter boarded his train would be the best place to do so. He would then be able to observe the Prince without the Prince seeing him.

I gave the note to one of my very interesting boarders—Motu by name—to deliver to the Colonel. I also asked him to buy one *imam-e-zamin*[2] on his way back and gave him a 10 rupee note for that purpose.

After that, I went to sleep. When I got up, it was noon. I had a wash and drank two cups of tea to get over my fatigue. Then I asked Motu about the errands I had entrusted him with. He said the Colonel had said I should have tea with him in the evening. 'But', Motu added, shamefacedly, 'I forgot the name of the article you had asked me to purchase on my way back. Kindly write it down on a slip of paper and I'll fetch it now.' I smiled away my anger at his stupidity and wrote down the name of the shop as well as the item.

At 4.00 I hired a taxi and reached Fani's house. He was surprised to see me so early since the train was to leave only at 7.00 p.m. I told him not to waste time but to get ready. In short, I picked up Fani and we reached the Colonel's house at exactly half past four. The Colonel was very happy to see us. He had so far only heard Fani's name. He was honoured to meet him in person. He thanked me profusely for bringing him to his house. Seating us in the drawing room, he shouted: 'Mastan Saab, Mastan Saab,' After a number of calls a voice responded from outside: 'Coming, Sir.' Presently a young boy of about 17 appeared before us. He was dark and had an English haircut. He looked like a vagabond. Mischief danced in his eyes. The Colonel spoke to him brusquely: 'Get a duster and clean the table. Also, tell Madam that the guests have come and to send tea immediately.' Mastan Saab brought a cheap thick towel, which did not seem to have been washed for months. The Colonel flew into a rage on seeing it. 'You swine,' he thundered, 'what is this rag you have brought. Get a proper duster.' Mastan Saab smiled sheepishly and ran inside. This time he brought a duster with which he wiped the table. Then he brought a tea service and put it on the table. There were two types of biscuits and two half-boiled eggs each for both of us. The Colonel poured tea for us and we drank 'Orange Pekoe' with our host.

There were three windows in the drawing room, all of which were closed. The Colonel ordered Mastan Saab to open all the windows and to tell the Madam to get out a clean shirt and *gudgi* (tight pajamas) from his box and to prepare his paan-box and wallet.

We finished tea in about ten minutes. Five minutes later the Colonel emerged dressed in a black sherwani, white pajamas, and a black cap. Mastan Saab brought the paan-box and wallet and put them on the table. The Colonel offered us a paan each and took one himself. Till 6.00 Fani and I enjoyed our host's peculiar speech. At exactly 6.00, we drove to Nampally railway station where over 200 cars were parked neatly in rows. I instructed the driver to park the car outside the gate at a convenient place because shortly we would be going to Begumpet station. Then I took the Colonel, crossed the steel gate, and reached the platform. There was still one hour for the train to arrive but already there were about 400 persons in formal dastar and bugloos, waiting to see off the Prince.

The Colonel exclaimed in wonder: 'Abbaba! So many Hindus, Muslims, Englishmen, and Parsis are gathered as if it is a fair.' I said: 'Colonel, you have seen nothing. For the last three days, noblemen and their children have been coming daily to the Hill Fort Palace to tie imam-e-zamins to the Prince's arms. So far, between 2000 and 4000, zamins would have been tied at the Palace. Here only those people have come who could not make it to the Palace. And there is still one hour for the train to come. From 6.30 high officials and leading nobles will start arriving and by 6.45 there won't be an inch of vacant space on the platform. There will be at least 1500 cars parked outside.

The Colonel exclaimed in wonder: 'Hasbanullah Naim-ul-wakil ....' Then he said to me: 'Tell me, there must be Rs 4000 to 5000 collected through the imam-e-zamins.'

'More,' I replied, 'At least Rs 6000 to 7000.'

The Colonel asked: 'Then how is that amount spent?' I said: 'Nawab Shaheed Yar Jung distributes it amongst the poor and indigent.' The Colonel said, cynically: 'That is all in theory. He must be giving only Rs 1000 to

1500 to the poor. Five to six thousand must be going into his pocket. You people must also be getting something. Forgive me, but I am a blunt person. Hasbanullah ....'

At 6.30 high officials, ministers, and nobles started arriving and by a quarter to seven the platform was overflowing with people. At 6.50 the Prince got down from his car. A hush fell over the crowd of about 7000. It was as if no one was there. Whichever way he passed, row after row of people were doing floor salaams to him. When one arm would be completely covered with imam-e-zamins, a servant would start taking them off. The well-wishers would then start tying them on the other arm. Countless garlands were put around the Prince's neck. He himself would take them off and go on handing them to an attendant.

At 6.55 whistles started blowing. That was the signal that His Exalted Highness the Nizam was coming. The Colonel took hold of my arm nervously and said, 'Let us run away from here. Otherwise, it will be difficult to get out. I am already feeling jittery.'

I said to him, 'Colonel, see the spectacle of the arrival of our ruler. The train has not yet come. It will stop here for at least ten minutes. That will give us enough time to reach Begumpet.'

The Colonel said, 'No, Baba, this spectacle is too much for me. My life is in danger. My heart is already pounding.' So saying, he dragged me towards the barricade. We jumped over it. Outside there were at least a thousand cars. We walked fast towards our car. Hardly had we got in, when the Nizam's car sped past us. I recited a couplet. By now the Colonel had recovered his composure. He said, 'Let's get going; then I shall also recite a couplet.' As the car started, Fani asked the Colonel for his piece. It was Fani's first meeting with the Colonel but when he heard the couplet, he could not control his laughter. The couplet was very funny and his explanation of it was funnier.

Soon we reached Begumpet. There were about a dozen members of the staff of the Prince who had come to say a quiet goodbye to him. I went in with Fani. Colonel Khan remained outside. As soon as we reached the platform, the train also steamed in. We rushed towards the saloon of the Prince. The attendant opened the door. Fani salaamed him first. I followed. Then I tied an imam-e-zamin. Fani followed. The Prince spoke kindly to us. Then he said, 'Now you can rest for three months. Because of me you could not sleep at night.'

I folded my hands and submitted respectfully: 'We are not worried about getting rest, Highness. What is gnawing at our hearts is that for a full ninety days we shall be deprived of acquiring the merit of keeping vigils.'

The Prince started laughing at my reply. Meanwhile the guard blew the whistle. We again salaamed, bade the Prince 'Khuda Hafiz', and got down from the train. The train started crawling. We salaamed from the platform. The engine hissed, belched out black smoke, and the train pulled out of sight.

Notes

FANI IN HYDERABAD DECCAN (PAGES 3–8)

[1] The Persian poet renowned for his quatrains, *The Rubaiyat*, translated into English by Edward Fitzgerald (1809–83).

THE FIRST NIGHT AT THE COURT (PAGES 8–18)

[1] A pair of two drums comprising a percussion instrument for Hindustani (north Indian) music.

[2] Here we are on difficult ground. This is technical point of Urdu poetry. The requirement of meter and rhyme are that the last part of every couplet in the ghazal should be in accordance with the phonetic value and syllables of '*Nazar Kyon nahin jate: Asar kyon nahin jate*'. Very often the discriminating audience anticipates this last part and is so struck by the excellence of thought or the height of craftsmanship that it utters it slightly before the singer and then breaks into spontaneous and vociferous praise in which others join and ask for an encore. This act of anticipation is a tribute both to the composer and to the one who anticipates it. The bathos of the incident, which follows, needs to be understood and enjoyed with this background.

THE SECOND NIGHT AT THE COURT (PAGES 18–25)

[1] This and the following couplets are not presented in translation, because that will not do justice to the original. Here the translator is up against a real difficulty and it seems advisable not to venture to attempt the task.

[2] The sixth Nizam, Mir Mahboob Ali Khan (1869–1911). He became a ruler at the age of three.

THE NIGHT OF EID (PAGES 25–33)

[1] Nazar: A customary offering to a prince or a noble on formal occasions like birthday or Eid. The minimum rate of this nazar was Rs 24 for the Nizam. It was less in the case of princes. Of course, there was no maximum limit as is the case with

any present. It was a regular source of income for the Nizam and became quite a scandal.

[2] Dry Indian bread, circular like the Mexican 'tortilla'.

[3] Shallow-fried bread made of wheat.

[4] Here the author seems to be confusing the name. The correct name was Jamaluddin. The description broadly fits him. However, he is not known to have written any poetry. For a detailed account of this character, see my book *Hyderabad: Memoirs of a City* (Hyderabad, Orient Longman, 1994). Also, my article 'The Wit-laureate of Hyderabad' published in *The Hindu*, 15 February 1998.

[5] Call for prayers for Muslims. It is made five times a day.

[6] The first month of the Muslim calendar. Held sacred because the martyrdom of Hussain, grandson of the Prophet, is mourned during this month. It is a month during which, among other things, fighting is prohibited.

[7] Born in UP in 1899. Came to Hyderabad in 1931. Started *Payam*, an Urdu daily, in 1933. A well-known journalist of nationalist leanings. Later, he became director of information in the government. He warned the Nizam of the consequences of not joining the Indian Union in 1947 and wrote a long letter to him before leaving Hyderabad in disgust. He died in 1955.

[8] Another well-known poet who came to Hyderabad from the north.

DECLINING A JOB (PAGES 33–40)

[1] Nawab Manzoor Jung was one of the seven Muslims who signed a statement on 13 August 1948 urging the Nizam to join the Indian Union. The Nizam was most upset and sent a note to the Nawab asking him to retract the statement. The Nawab received the royal epistle with due courtesy—he touched it with his eyes and kissed it before opening it—but he refused to budge from his stand.

[2] Nawab Sir Mehdi Yar Jung (1882–1948). His original name was Syed Mehdi Hussain Bilgrami. He was the fourth son of Imadul-Mulk (Syed Hussain Bilgrami—see prologue). He was a graduate in English literature from Oxford. He first served in the Education Department and rose to be Secretary of the Political Department and then a Minister of the Political and Education Departments. He retired as President of the Council of Ministers in 1946 and died two years later.

[3] The allusion is to Hussain, the grandson of the Prophet and one of the five sacred personages for Shia Muslims. Mehdi Yar Jung was a Shia.

THE CURSE OF ALCOHOL (PAGES 40–6)

[1] He sported the pen name of 'Mir'. He was a resident of district Partap Garh and was headmaster of an English medium middle school. Apart from English, he was well versed in Persian and Arabic. His hobbies were to prepare amulets, nullify the evil eye, and play the sitar and chess. He was an expert in astrology and wrote

good poetry quite frequently. Now for sometime, he has been inclined towards Sufism. He is 87. He does not acknowledge Josh as a poet and calls his poetry all sorts of names. For about 40 years, he has been staying at the shrine of Shah Abdul Rehman at Lucknow. (Author's note).

[2] Sir Akbar Hydari who came to Hyderabad as an officer in the Accounts Department. He rose to succeed Maharaja Kishen Pershad as Prime Minister which post he occupied from 1936 to 1941. Thereafter he was appointed Member of the Viceroy's Executive Council but died before he could take it up.

THE HORSEMANSHIP OF DAGH (PAGES 52–60)

[1] For a detailed account of his appointment as poetic instructor to the sixth Nizam, see my book *Memoirs of a City* (Hyderabad, Orient Longman, 1995).

[2] Sheikh Sharf-ud-din Shirazi, the famous poet of Persian who wrote the classics *Gulistan* and *Bostan*. 'Saadi' is his poetic name.

IRANI'S URDU (PAGES 60–5)

[1] Mir Taqi Mir (1722–1810) and Mirza Mohammad Rafi Sauda (1713–80) were two great masters of Urdu poetry of the eighteenth century.

[2] The people of Hyderabad State were called *mulki* (natives) while those from outside the State, particularly the north, were called Hindustani (from Hindustan or India).

[3] Abul Hasan Tana Shah, the last Qutb Shahi ruler of Golconda (1672–87), was known for his sybaritic lifestyle. He spent the last fourteen years of his life in captivity after his defeat at the hands of Aurangzeb in 1687.

[4] Literally, it means 'which blow should I take and from which should I save myself'. But there is a potential for a smutty pun here. The Iranians, like the French, cannot pronounce the hard 't' (as in chat). They can only pronounce the soft 't'. When that is done, 'chot' acquires the meaning of the female sex organ. The reader can thus imagine what the couplet would then come to mean.

[5] Here again there is a pun based upon the inability of the Irani to utter the hard 't'. 'Maratha' thus become 'marata' which in Urdu means, 'Are you willing to commit sodomy?'

THE DECCANI COLONEL BLIMP (PAGES 65–8)

[1] According to some, this character is based on the late Colonel Zain-ul-Abdeen Khan of the Nizam's private estate, called *Sarf-e-khas*. The engaging quality of this chapter is the use of Dakhni, native to the people of Hyderabad but so amusing in its syntax and pronunciation of common words in Urdu. Unfortunately, that cannot be brought out in translation.

[2] It is an *ayat* (verse) from the Quran (3:173). It means: 'For us God suffices and He is the best dispenser of affairs.' It was a cant phrase used by the Colonel in his conversation.

[3] The uniqueness of this chapter lies in the Dakhni language, which the Colonel used in his conversation.

NAWAB SHAHAB JUNG (PAGES 69–75)

[1] This fall from favour is related to the succession of Mir Osman Ali Khan as the seventh Nizam. His succession was not fully accepted by many nobles due to the alleged illegitimacy of his birth. (His mother was allegedly already pregnant when the sixth Nizam took her into wedlock.) The story goes that Shahab Jung offered to have the nobles terrorized into submission by a mock show of the temper of the new ruler in the court. It was agreed between them that one day Shahab Jung would come late to court and the Nizam would pull him up just to show that he was in control. It so happened that while the drama was being enacted the young Nizam became really angry and abused Shahab Jung excessively. Thereupon Shahab Jung felt so humiliated that he withdrew into his mansion and never showed up again in public. See my book *Memoirs of a City*.

ROYAL LARGESSE (PAGES 75–9)

[1] A dish made of pulse and rice boiled together and tempered with clarified butter and spices. It is not a formal dish in the north but is cooked as a delicacy and relished in the Deccan.

[2] Mirza Asadullah Khan 'Ghalib' (1779–1869), the best-known Urdu poet of India. His poems are sung and enjoyed even today by all.

[3] Moulana Altaf Hussain Hali (1837–1914), renowned poet, critic, essayist in Urdu, and a thinker.

[4] The long poem is omitted in the translation. It is not likely to interest anyone except those versed in very esoteric Urdu.

THE DEPARTURE OF BEGUM AKHTAR (PAGES 80–3)

[1] One of the three types of Hindustani classical music popular today. It is lyrical in nature, based on *shringar ras* (the sentiment of romance and love), which spans a total range of expression from the sensuous to the sublime.

[2] Sarangi is considered the most important of bowed string instruments in the north Indian music. Its sound is closest to the human voice and so is used at once both as a typical folk and concert lute.

[3] It works out to Rs 20.57 million. Here the author's memory seems to be playing tricks with him. The trust was established much later, on 8 October 1949,

and its corpus was Rs 1,82,00,000 (Rs 18.2 million). The trust for the Senior Prince was set up on 8 January 1950 with a similar corpus. The amount was invested in the securities of the Government of India. The Prince was to get interest at 1 per cent plus an annuity from the corpus adding up to Rs 600,000 per annum for life.

RAGGING PIYA (PAGES 83–6)

[1] *Sura* 36 of the Quran. It is called the heart of the Quran and it is believed that if it is recited just before the death of a person, his suffering is reduced and death becomes easy.

[2] Colonel Waghray (1902–72) of the Indian Medical Service of the Army was a leading physician of Hyderabad. He was attached to the Nizam and his household as a personal physician.

THE PRINCE GOES TO EUROPE (PAGES 86–90)

[1] Nampally is the main railway station of Hyderabad, Begumpet is a small flag station about 3 km from it. It was generally used for VIPs to board trains privately.

[2] An armband made of shiny colourful cloth. Some coins or currency notes are stitched into its fold. It is tied on the arm of the person who is proceeding on a journey with wishes and prayers for his safe return. On returning, the person gives away the money in charity by way of thanksgiving. It is a very touching custom of Hyderabad.